School Leadership

Case Studies Solving School Problems

Second Edition

Benjamin Piltch and Terrence Quinn

ROWMAN & LITTLEFIELD EDUCATION
A division of
ROWMAN & LITTLEFIELD PUBLISHERS, INC.
Lanham • New York • Toronto • Plymouth. UK

Published by Rowman & Littlefield Education
A division of Rowman & Littlefield Publishers, Inc.
A wholly owned subsidary of The Rowman & Littlefield Publishing Group, Inc.
4501 Forbes Boulevard, Suite 200, Lanham, Maryland 20706
http://www.rowmaneducation.com

Estover Road, Plymouth PL6 7PY, United Kingdom

British Library Cataloguing in Publication Information Available

Library of Congress Cataloging-in-Publication Data

Piltch, Benjamin.
  School leadership : case studies solving school problems / Benjamin Piltch and Terrence Quinn. -- 2nd ed.
    p. cm.
ISBN 978-1-60709-951-2 (cloth : alk. paper) -- ISBN 978-1-60709-952-9 (pbk. : alk. paper) -- ISBN 978-1-60709-953-6 (electronic)
  1. School management and organization--United States--Case studies. 2. Educational leadership--United States--Case studies. 3. Problem solving--United States--Case studies. 4. Decision making--United States--Case studies. I. Quinn, Terrence, 1946- II. Title.
  LB2805.P589 2011
  371.2--dc22
                                                          2010033057

Printed in the United States of America

Contents

Preface

It is a truism that U.S. education is changing, and with it, the job description of school leaders is also changing. Whereas in the past, a good school was viewed as one that was orderly, quiet, and well run, today that description has become passé. A good school administrator was seen as someone who knew school management principles, could balance a budget and schedule classes, and could handle paperwork with some degree of efficiency. Today's school leader, on the other hand, must be able to work collaboratively with the entire school community to develop a positive learning environment and maintain a high standard of student achievement. The job today requires an entirely new skill set that includes knowledge of the use of data as a tool to improve school planning, familiarity with new instructional methods, accountability standards, and certainly the ability to do more with less.

In this second edition, we are cognizant of the changes in the job description of school administrators and have introduced new case studies and ideas that reflect new school leadership models for the twenty-first century. These new case studies, like those of the first edition, challenge the reader to reflect on an ever-expanding variety of complex issues. Increasingly, these issues revolve around such vexing dilemmas as motivation of senior faculty, new paradigms of professional development, conflict resolution, more effective leadership styles conducive to human resource management trends, among others.

As veteran teachers, principals, administrators, and college professors with a collective experience of a half century in educational administration in various and diverse settings from poor urban areas to affluent suburban communities, we feel that we have much to offer new and veteran administrators as well as the inquiring public.

In particular, we feel that by sharing some of our experiences in a case study format, we are able to bring focus to some of the many problems, issues, and leadership challenges that today's schools and school administrators are facing.

Targeted audiences for our book include aspiring and practicing school principals and assistant principals, college professors working with candidates for degrees in school leadership, and superintendents, assistant superintendents, and others responsible for the in-service education of administrators.

In addition, we see our book as a tool for the general public (including teachers, concerned parents, and community leaders) with an interest in education to gain insight into the problems and possible solutions to current educational issues.

By sharing some of our experiences, we believe that the case studies lend themselves to thoughtful discussion of actions taken and not taken, as well as alternative strategies to deal with the issues raised. The users of this book will be given ample opportunity to experience many dilemmas faced by real administrators and thoughtfully decide the proper course(s) of action that might positively address these dilemmas.

This book is intended to share the reality of educational leadership with those who are considering or beginning on this road or looking for insights into educational decision making and problem solving. Hopefully it will be a useful tool in the preparation and professional development of school leaders.

Chapter One

Twenty-First-Century School Leadership: Best Practices

Shortly after the retirement of its principal, the Port Valley Central School began the recruitment and selection process for a new school head. A hiring committee of teachers, parents, support personnel, and a student council representative determined the new principal should be a person who espoused, and practiced, leadership standards for the twenty-first century as enunciated by the Interstate School Leaders Licensure Consortium (ISLLC) (www.wallacefoundation.org). These ISLLC standards, developed in cooperation with major education organizations, call for a school vision; a vibrant teaching-learning culture; a collaborative working environment; awareness of, and sensitivity to, community needs; understanding of the political and cultural dynamic of schools, and attention to ethical ideals.

The committee was charged with the responsibility to generate a set of comprehensive selection criteria that would measure leadership skills as articulated by the ISLLC standards. Further, the committee was tasked with other significant criteria including ascertaining an applicant's educational philosophy, a record of educational achievement, administrative experience, knowledge of instruction and curriculum, familiarity with the use of data as a tool to guide instruction, and oral and written communication skills.

The committee used an assortment of activities to measure the various criteria. A list of the activities included requiring a complete, achievement-oriented résumé and cover letter as minimum requirements before candidates would receive further review. The committee proceeded to narrow the applicant pool based on this initial screening of résumés. A telephone interview with several candidates resulted in a further narrowing of the pool.

Finally, the committee agreed that four candidates would submit to an all-day round of meetings designed to familiarize them with the workings of the

1

school. The committee organized a working lunch with various constituent groups, a tour of the school community, writing sample, and a one-hour interview. This was all followed by a review of references.

After further deliberation, the committee decided that two applicants, Marie Salvato and Kate Redmond, would become finalists for the position of principal. Each presented herself as well qualified for the principalship. Each articulated a progressive educational philosophy with a proven record of accomplishment and a thorough knowledge of curriculum, professional development, and instructional methodology. Each possessed a keen sense of the power of data to improve student achievement.

After some discussion, the committee decided to ask Marie and Kate to conduct a one-hour meeting with the Port Valley Central School Planning Council. Kate and Marie were asked to present their philosophies, vision for the school, initiatives to encourage a positive learning culture, plans for community involvement, and their ideas to cultivate a collaborative decision-making system for the school.

Marie was her usual highly polished and articulate self as she shared with the Planning Council her educational background at a renowned Ivy League university and her current pursuit of a doctorate in education. She began: "I want to talk to you and tell you my plans for Port Valley. My philosophy is borne of an intense desire to improve student success, which remains the cornerstone of each of the ISLLC standards. My vision for Port Valley is based on the groundbreaking work of some researchers who pioneered innovative ideas in this area. My plans for a positive teaching-learning environment can only be accomplished through a commitment on the part of all of us to demand the highest expectations for student achievement. Education for the children is too vital for any of us to fail in this effort. For those who may not meet the challenge of high expectations, I promise to support you through close and tight supervision that will help you attain school goals. We can only reach our targets through collaboration and confidence in one another. We will collaborate after I decide the best plan of action. With my established record of educational leadership, I will not fail you." For the next half hour or so, Marie continued to outline her plans for Port Valley. At the end of the allotted time, she submitted to a few questions.

Next, Kate Redmond met with the Planning Council. "Good afternoon, ladies and gentlemen, I want to thank you for giving me the opportunity to talk with you about ideas to strengthen an already strong school here at Port Valley. The school's recent success is a tribute to your skill and devotion. You are the resident experts and if I am selected to serve as your principal, be assured I will use your talents and experiences to ensure an achieving school where success includes student achievement, the professional growth of faculty, and community participation in decision making. Having met with numerous school representatives, I think you already know my educational background, my professional experiences, and my philosophy. I would prefer to spend the bulk of this presentation time talking with you and listening to your ideas, and working to create a trusting work atmosphere. I hope you do not mind if I take notes to help me follow up if I am ultimately selected as your principal."

After some initial hesitation, Planning Council members shared some accomplishments, current concerns and issues, and their own priorities for the future of Port Valley. Kate listened attentively as she took copious notes of their remarks, asked clarifying questions, and offered "several approaches that worked for me in the past and may be worth considering at Port Valley."

QUESTIONS

1. Discuss and evaluate the selection criteria developed by the Port Valley Central School hiring committee.
2. How should the committee measure the criteria for principal selection?
3. What indicators would you seek to examine on the candidates' résumé and cover letter?
4. Evaluate the leadership styles of the two finalists for the position of principal.

COMMENTS

Effective school leadership for the twenty-first century emphasizes knowledge of data, assessment, program implementation, curriculum and instruction, and professional development. Candidates seeking to become school leaders would do well to develop a thorough grounding in all of these areas of supervision and school management. The ISLLC standards serve as a useful resource to enhance one's professional preparation in the field of school leadership.

The hiring committee at Port Valley Central School has certainly developed a comprehensive list of criteria that will allow for a variety of information as it conducts its business. As thorough as the criteria may be, the difficulty here is its ability to assess accurately the knowledge and skills of the candidates. How can the committee know with any great certainty whether the applicants are sensitive to the community needs or that their approaches to supervision represent an enlightened philosophy? The subjective nature of interviews is well known and may be designed more to determine their interpersonal skills rather than their potential for future job success.

Nonetheless, the committee can ensure a wise final decision if it has undergone training in the legal implications of its questions. For example, many typical queries relating to age ("How old are you?"), marital status ("Are you married? If not, are you living with someone?"), residence ("Do you own or rent?"), health ("Are you planning to have a family?"), criminal record ("Have you ever been arrested?"), and religion are potentially discriminatory and could be the basis for litigation.

The committee would be wise to use an interview rating form that consists of a matrix to compare candidate responses. At the same time the committee would be well served if it designs a standard set of questions for all applicants and an accompanying rubric that highlights model responses. Keeping accurate records of candidate responses would be helpful in later conversations and provide an audit mechanism in the event a candidate sues. These techniques take the subjectivity out of the interview process and replace it with more objective, job-related measurements.

While the hiring committee is pursuing its tasks, members should know that numerous educational leadership professional associations provide a plethora of resources to assist in the supervisory selection process. For example, the National Association for Secondary School Principals (NASSP) runs an assessment center in which a team of trained assessors review and rate prospective supervisors who submit to a variety of job-related activities. These activities include instructional leadership, resolving complex problems, communication, and developing oneself and others. The NASSP has produced a set of "21st Century School Administrator Skills," which are described on their web page "21st Century School Administrator Skills Self-Assessment and Observer Assessment."

With respect to the choice of Marie Salvato and Kate Redmond as finalists, the committee demonstrated its sophistication when it requested that both applicants conduct a meeting with the Planning Council. This approach enabled the committee to view Marie's and Kate's obvious interpersonal skills and, more importantly, their very different leadership styles.

Based on her comments to the Planning Council, Marie appears decisive, assertive, direct, and brimming with energy and ideas. Marie is more task-oriented, while Kate is more people-oriented. For the Planning Council, the issue is whether Kate's collaborative approach can achieve the desired results.

Views on effective leadership have changed in recent years. Whereas in the past leadership was believed to be a function of task accomplishment and a capacity to take charge and complete the assignment, more recent research emphasizes the importance of the "people factor" in attaining goals. This view encourages participation by employees in establishing a vision for the organization and in the decision-making process. A critical element of the effective leader is the ability to work with and through employees to pursue common objectives. What is needed is to find ways to work with the entire school community to develop collaborative goals about teaching and learning. This approach is more likely to empower faculty to become more focused and energized about school issues.

Talented leaders understand the pivotal role they play in helping others maximize their potential. They spend considerable amounts of time nurturing employee talent and communicating the mission throughout the organization because they know mutually supported goals create a higher level of responsibility.

Marie's approach seems to encompass a preference for structure, closed decision-making, top-down leadership, and careful monitoring of teacher performance. For Marie it may be difficult to develop teacher talent because of her direct supervisory style. Her comments to the Planning Council clearly illustrate her philosophy of supervision and her approaches to school issues.

Kate's approach, on the other hand, seems to promote a collaborative, joint problem-solving effort in which school leaders and faculty talk, observe, listen, assess, and respond in a more shared decision approach. With this method Kate is seen as a transformational leader in her efforts to involve teachers in goal setting and help them pursue a more congenial professional school culture.

Kate may be the more preferred candidate for the principalship of Port Valley Central School. How then can she capitalize on her likely appointment as the new principal and enhance her transformational leadership style to advance the goals of her school?

Some early researchers (Leithwood and Jantzi 1990; Poplin 1992; Quinn 2005; Sagor 1992) who introduced new concepts of transformational leadership offer several practice strategies that Kate should consider:

- Be visible every day by visiting classrooms and giving support.
- Initiate a professional development program that would include intervisitations, mentoring, critical friends group, a buddy system, and demonstration lessons.
- Involve staff in developing school goals, vision, and priorities at the beginning of each school year and reviewing throughout.
- Let teachers experiment with new teaching ideas. Share and discuss research with them.
- Use action research teams or school improvement committees as a way of sharing power.
- Find the good things that are happening and publicly recognize the work of staff and students who have helped to improve the school.
- Survey the staff often about their professional needs. Be receptive to teacher attitudes and philosophies.

- Have high expectations for all faculty but don't expect 100 percent if you are not also committed to your own high expectations.

These practices may be quite useful for Kate as she begins her career as principal of Port Valley Central School because numerous studies have indicated that such a leadership style can have significant influence on teacher collaboration. For example, Sagor (1992) found that schools that reported having a transformational leader as principal were more likely to have a culture conducive to a more positive teaching-learning environment.

For more on transformational leadership and a comprehensive review of the research, see the work of Bernard Bass and Ronald Riggio (2006).

REFERENCES

Bass, Bernard, and Ronald Riggio. 2006. *Transformational leadership*, 2nd ed. Mahwah, NJ: Erlbaum.

Leithwood, Kenneth, and Doris Jantzi. 1990. Transformational leadership: How principals can help school cultures. Paper presented at the annual meeting of the Canadian Association for Curriculum Studies, June 12–15, in Victoria, British Columbia.

National Association for Secondary School Principals. 21st Century School Administrator Skills Self-Assessment and Observer Assessment. Available at www.Principals.org/ProfessionalDevelopment/NASSP/LeadershipSkillsAssessment.aspx.

Poplin, Mary. 1992. The leader's new role: Looking to the growth of teachers. *Educational Leadership* 49 (5): 11–12.

Quinn, Terrence. 2005. How principals impact teacher retention. *Academic Exchange Quarterly* 9 (2): 225–229.

Sagor, Richard. 1992. Three principals who make a difference. *Educational Leadership* 49 (5): 13–18.

Chapter Two

Talent Multipliers — and Diminishers

Westin Square School District Superintendent Jason Thomas was pleased with the final selection and appointment of Loretta Long and Karen Trent as the new principals of Springfield School and the Bell Avenue School, respectively.

Both Loretta and Karen had strong records of achievement in their previous positions. Loretta had been the longtime director of a major curriculum improvement program in another state. Karen had served as assistant principal in a neighboring school district. Both appeared to be knowledgeable about current trends in education, and both exuded significant skills necessary for their success.

In addition, the Springfield School and the Bell Avenue School were quite similar in many respects. They both enjoyed similar student success on standardized achievement tests. Faculty motivation and involvement in school activities at Springfield and Bell Avenue were flourishing, and parent participation in school decision making was extensive.

Upon completion of their first year performance as principals, Superintendent Thomas reviewed longitudinal data for both schools and observed results that were not at all similar. Under Loretta's leadership, for example, Springfield witnessed a student enrollment increase. Teachers were writing grants and publishing articles in professional journals. Learning environment surveys conducted by the superintendent's office were more positive than in previous years. Graduation rates were on the upswing. Community support for school initiatives was apparent to all observers.

Bell Avenue School, however, seemed to experience higher than normal teacher turnover rates. There was an uptick in grievances against Karen and the administrative leadership team she put together immediately after her appointment as principal. Student enrollment suffered a mild decline. Teacher leadership was not evident. Graduation rates dipped slightly, and parent participation in school activities was missing.

After a careful review of the data and a series of interviews and meetings with his own staff who served as resource agents for both schools, Superintendent Thomas noticed a difference in leadership styles between Loretta and Karen. Loretta supported faculty in their willingness to take risks and become creative in their teaching. "How can I help you to do your job better?" was her usual greeting to teachers and staff.

Karen was more careful and controlling in faculty efforts to assume leadership projects. For example, teachers who were eager to write grants, publish in journals, and present their curriculum innovations at local conferences were reminded that activities should be cleared with Karen's office "so I can give you my own professional expertise in the direction you wish to undertake."

QUESTIONS

1. What other factors might Superintendent Thomas use to evaluate both principals during and after their first years of service as principals in the Westin Square School District?
2. How would you assess the leadership styles of Loretta and Karen?
3. What specific advice would you offer to Loretta and Karen to enhance their management capabilities?

COMMENTS

The importance of leadership as a variable in school improvement has been documented elsewhere in this book. In the case of the Springfield School and the Bell Avenue School, both principals had previously demonstrated a capacity for leadership in terms of proactive decision-making skills, knowledge of school operations, and strategic planning sagacity.

In our discussion of their leadership traits, the research of Liz Wiseman and Greg McKeown is instructive. Writing in the *Harvard Business Review*, they remind us that "some leaders drain all the intelligence and capability out of their teams. Because they often need to be the smartest, most capable person in the room, these managers shut down the smarts of others, ultimately stifling the flow of ideas" (2010, 117).

In her controlling, highly prescriptive approach to faculty supervision, Karen may inadvertently be weakening the talent pool that has existed at Bell Avenue School. She may be discouraging the exchange of ideas and faculty growth by her eagerness to give them her own professional expertise so willingly. Such a philosophy of managing people contributes to dominating the thinking of employees and underutilizes their potential as creative workers and problem solvers.

Wiseman and McKeown note that managers fall into two separate areas with different traits, attitudes, and philosophies. Each has an impact on the productivity of the organization. They classify these managers as diminishers and multipliers. They identify five types of manager diminishers:

- empire builders who hoard resources and underutilize talent;
- tyrants who create a tense environment that suppresses people's thinking and capabilities, which produces straitjacketed thinking;
- know-it-alls who need to show off their knowledge;
- autocratic decision makers who make abrupt decisions that confuse everyone;
- micromanagers who need to be involved in everything.

Manager multipliers, on the other hand, promote a work environment that cultivates intelligence and problem-solving abilities on the part of employees. These managers expect, and encourage, staff to use their own skills and experiences to devise solutions to workplace issues. Wiseman and McKeown offer five kinds of manager multipliers:

- talent magnets who attract capable people and use them to their highest potential;
- liberators who create an intense environment that requires people's best thinking and work;
- challengers who define an opportunity that makes people stretch their thinking and behavior;
- debate makers who drive sound decisions by cultivating rigorous debates;
- leaders who give employees ownership of results and invest in their success.

It would appear that Loretta might be classified as a natural multiplier. This certainly is not the case with Karen, nor with so many other leaders today who fall somewhere between the natural multiplier and the manager prone to diminish employee capability. Fortunately, Wiseman and McKeown offer advice for those managers who seek to enhance faculty potential:

1. Hire talent: Hiring and managing a quality staff is the most important task facing administrators, and certainly none more so than in schools. In his widely acclaimed book *Good to Great* (2001, 41) the management expert Jim Collins refers to this task as "getting the right people on the bus."

Once hired, that employee must be supported and connected with other talented employees to create symbiotic energy and ideas.

2. Foster a productive work environment: Smart managers encourage the free flow of ideas and see conflicts of ideas as healthy. From such group interaction, new and better decisions emanate. An ancillary benefit of this process is a higher degree of ownership.

3. Execute wisely: The multipliers see themselves more as coaches and mentors than as executives. They encourage others to develop decision-making skills and delegate often to staff. In doing so they engage further in talent development.

In this case, it is obvious that Karen is a talent diminisher, however reluctant she may be to accept that characterization. How can Karen develop a multiplier mindset? A few suggestions:

1. Offer public recognition to faculty and applaud their efforts, if not their results.

2. Practice MBWA (manage by wandering around). Visit staff throughout the school building and express interest in, and support for, their work.

3. Lead by example. Implement ideas of faculty, not simply express appreciation for their innovative ideas.

4. Listen to employees. The adage reminds us there are reasons people have two ears and one mouth—so we listen twice as much as we speak. If Karen listens more carefully, she might earn respect from faculty.

5. Involve faculty in school issues over which they have knowledge or responsibility.

6. Be sympathetic to employee concerns. This will demonstrate to faculty that Karen understands their needs and will use her authority to resolve these matters.

REFERENCES

Collins, Jim. 2001. *Good to great*. New York: HarperCollins.
Wiseman, Liz, and Greg McKeown. 2010. Bringing out the best in your people. *Harvard Business Review* 88 (5): 117–121.

Chapter Three

Is Test Practice Effective Instruction?

Since the late 1970s, test practice has been controversial. It has been proven that understanding the format of a test is helpful in performing somewhat better on tests. However, when a county, district, or school overemphasizes test preparation time, teachers and parents complain that "teaching to the Test is not effective instruction."

How then does a school system incorporate test practice into its curriculum so that the teachers and parents are content while at the same time maximizing the results for students? Whether we call it test practice, test sophistication, or test preparation, it has become a part of every school's instructional program for preparing the pupils for testing. Please notice that we specify *part of the instructional program* because test preparation is only one aspect of a quality educational program.

In the Eisenhower School District Superintendent Carmen Rodriguez hired a former school administrator to set up a countywide testing program that would hopefully result in higher test scores for the students. Superintendent Rodriguez was under enormous pressure to improve the test scores, and she was determined to please the entire community. She gave the responsibility to Sandra Stewart to "mobilize the county's schools so that the literacy test scores improve."

At the first school board meeting in September, Superintendent Rodriguez introduced the new testing coordinator Sandra Stewart to the audience and asked her to give an orientation to the attendees about her plans for test preparation for the schools. Sandra's words were remarkable for being refreshing and sensitive to each school in the county.

She began by saying that she is going to listen to each school staff discuss its present test preparation program. She is also going to go to the state education department meetings about testing to turnkey to the county's schools information about the most up-to-date format of the upcoming state exams. She will also provide the schools with the format for the countywide tests to be given in all the schools. Next Sandra explained that this entire process is going to include the advice and recommendations of the county's school administrators and the teachers. At the end of the process she plans to survey all the constituents including the parents and the students to ascertain how smoothly and efficiently it went. The audience was delightfully stunned. Never before had anyone said that the administrators and teachers would be fully involved in the initial development of a program. Usually it was handed down from up high and they were to implement it. Sometimes sufficient funds accompanied the requested changes, and often the mandates were unfunded.

Mrs. Tina Saunders, the parent of a gifted student, wanted to know if the test practice program was going to erase or limit the innovative teaching of the higher-level thinking skills her child has been learning. Sandra responded saying that it absolutely would not. "As a matter of fact, I plan to encourage the teaching of higher-level thinking skills for all students not for just the gifted students."

"How can the test preparation be added to the high school curriculum, which is already overloaded and there is little time for anything new?" asked Mark Babbett, principal of the Eleanor Roosevelt High School. "I plan to sit down with all the high school principals and with the assistant principals and teacher's representatives and find time to integrate test preparation into the school's program. Perhaps the English teachers can do it for the literacy tests. Maybe we can find a zero period for it. In any case let's work together to see how it can be done."

Principal Babbett seemed satisfied with this response.

"Will you do the same for the middle schools?" asked Maria Rios, principal of the Winthrop Middle School. "Absolutely," Sandra answered.

"We have superb teachers, schedules and flexible programs in the elementary schools. Our students do well on tests. Do we have to have test practice?" asked Principal Margaret Hayes of the Marlboro Elementary School.

"Yes, everyone must do test practice. It has been shown to help students. Those who do not have any understanding of the format usually do worse than they could have if they had knowledge of the format of the tests. However, I will be working with everyone to incorporate these practices in a realistic non-overwhelming fashion," Sandra remarked.

Everyone seemed satisfied and left the meeting thinking, "Will we really see our input be respected as we move forward?"

QUESTIONS

1. Why would the audience consider this meeting refreshing?
2. How can Sandra develop a test preparation program that will be satisfactory to the teachers, parents, and students and still incorporate effective instruction?
3. How can a test preparation program be implemented within a reasonable time and in a professional, comprehensive, thorough, and effective manner?

The audience considered this school board meeting refreshing because the new test coordinator made it clear from the onset in front of the board and the superintendent that she was going to involve each constituency in the planning for the new program. Sandra intended to get them to take ownership of the new process and procedures from the very beginning.

In some counties and districts it has been the practice to develop a program and then tell the school staff about it. Yet they were given the responsibility for implementing it successfully. One of the concerns that this county staff could have is will she follow through with what she stated to the audience at this school board meeting? Also, will the necessary monies to purchase the test practice materials be made available? Will there really be an understanding that each school has a different chemistry and programs? The plan may require tweaking to make it successful in each and every school.

Sandra should next visit the schools. In the morning she could visit one school and in the afternoon another until she visited every school in the county. In each school, she can ask what that school has been doing for test sophistication in the past. She may wish to ask what materials were used and how much time was taken for test practice in the past. She should also ask about its literacy program. What materials have been used? How much time has the school been using for literacy instruction? What innovative, exciting methods do the teachers use to motivate students about reading, writing, listening, and speaking?

She may wish to ask about the higher-level thinking skills and who gets the higher-level thinking skills instruction. She might ask if social studies and science reading materials were used within the literacy program. Another possible inquiry would be to ask whether stories are analyzed, such as through instruction about the characters, the setting, and story development.

Many in the schools may wonder why she is asking about these programs. They may be concerned that she is going to try to reduce programs or eliminate them to increase time for test preparation. School staffs often worry that creativity and innovation are forced out and replaced with boring test practice.

Sandra should meet with the principal and assistant principal, if there is one, and with several teachers and assure them that test preparation need not supplant good, exciting teaching and learning. If parents are available she should speak to them too. If she has an opportunity to speak with students, she could also gain insight into their school experiences.

Soon after her initial meetings, perhaps on a superintendent's conference day, she could divide the day's events into two parts. In the morning the topic could be "Effective Instruction." In the afternoon the topic could be "Test Preparation." The elementary school teachers could be placed in a room by grade level taught and the specialist out-of-the-classroom teachers could meet as a group. The middle school and the high school teachers could be gathered together by the subjects they teach.

The morning agenda could be set based upon the previous discussions within the schools. The participants might be delighted by the agenda and may even recognize a topic as one discussed earlier in a meeting in their own school.

Items on the agenda could include innovative instruction, model discipline strategies while teaching, and ongoing diagnosis to determine pupil progress of precisely what was taught. Many suggestions should be shared about integrating social studies and science nonfiction readings within the literacy program. Many of the techniques discussed should be related to the type of skills and processes that would be needed to master the future tests.

Topics such as the study of stories and comparisons of characters could be discussed and how to teach pupils to understand character development and seeing the significance of the setting as well as themes. The difference here is that instead of using the rigid format of tests, the teachers would be free to use motivating methods they themselves love to employ. For most of the year the teachers would be able to teach with creativity and high pupil involvement. They certainly should understand that the appropriate curriculum would be followed.

In addition to having turnkey staff members lead the workshops, selected teachers and administrators, who have utilized successful techniques, could model these strategies. Since they work in the county or district and have established their credibility, their sharing what has worked would be impressive to their colleagues.

After lunch everyone should be requested to go to the same previously designated rooms. The same individuals who led the morning meetings should lead the afternoon meetings. Only this time the agenda should be "Test Preparation" within the parameters of the total school program. The workshop leaders should have met with Sandra and worked out a meeting agenda that included an understanding of the importance of test sophistication.

The participants should be brought up to date with the format of the tests to be given in the late winter and spring. In addition a realistic timeframe for test practice should be weaved within the instruction.

Sandra could use the afternoon workshop to discuss when the test preparation should take place and how much is necessary. Her turnkey leaders could also discuss what test practice consists of. In schools where the test results have consistently been high there may be less test practice than those in which the students might require more time to master the format of tests.

In the gifted classes, it might take three or four weeks to instruct the students in the format of the tests. In a class with severe underachievers it might take three months. One strategy the workshop leaders could present follows.

On Monday the teachers present the format as they go over a commercially produced test and go step-by-step explaining and modeling how to take a test. They go into great detail about each element of the format. On Tuesday and Wednesday the students and the teacher can do the same together, with the students taking a more active role. On Thursday the students could take the dominant role with the teacher correcting, explaining, and embellishing what the students have to say. On Friday the students could practice on the commercially produced test while the teacher proctors as he or she would on the real test. The workshop leaders could then explain what to do after the tests are marked and plan instruction to correct weaknesses.

During the workshop the workshop leaders should review the do's and don'ts of test practice and test taking. Also the workshop leaders need to remind everyone present that they are to never use actual tests unless it is specifically stated that that particular test will never be used in the future.

Also do's and don'ts need to be clearly established as to the proctor's role during the tests as what help they may give to the students. They may, for example, replace a pencil or pen but may never give any hints or help with regard to the test. Also the do's and don'ts should be mentioned as to how proctors handle the tests once they are completed and how they get them to the county or central office safe and sound without ever being compromised.

Chapter Four

Zachary's Achilles' Heel

SUPE AXED: CONTRACT NOT RENEWED . *The Carville Crusader*, the local newspaper, trumpeted headlines about the failure of the Carville Board of Education to renew the contract of its superintendent Zachary Worthington. In a statement to the press about the nonrenewal, Board President Eileen Smithers stated, "The Board of Education thanks Zachary for his years of service to our children and our community. Under his leadership, pupil achievement rose consistently and we can count on numerous high school seniors to win college scholarships to prestigious universities. We wish him well in his future endeavors."

Effusive in its praise of the superintendent's service to Carville, the statement was strangely quiet about whatever drove the Board of Education to reject a new contract for Zachary. There had been no scandal attached to his name. He was hardly near retirement age. There had been no significant policy differences between Zachary and his employers. Schools were functioning well. The community did not rally around their departing superintendent but, in fact, seemed to support the board's decision by its acceptance of the move.

So what was the Achilles' heel that toppled Zachary? Privately board members admitted that their superintendent, a sincere and trustworthy individual, never developed the interpersonal skills the board felt were necessary to ensure his own professional success and the success of Carville schools. His failure to engage in active outreach to the community had caused the district schools to suffer. To cite a few examples, the Board of Education members suffered annual anxiety at the time of the school budget vote. On at least two occasions during Zachary's seven years of service as superintendent, the taxpayers rejected the budget. On another occasion it squeaked by with barely a dozen votes. To make matters worse, a major bond referendum that would have provided for more school construction to alleviate overcrowding in Carville elementary schools had also been defeated.

Other complaints about Zachary began to surface. Parents who raised questions at public Board of Education meetings rarely received answers from Zachary or from members of his staff. When the *Crusader* published articles about the schools, the stories would invariably include a sentence, "Schools Superintendent Zachary Worthington was unavailable for comment." Other times stories would state, "The superintendent did not return repeated phone calls from this newspaper."

Eileen and her board colleagues were determined that a major qualification for the new superintendent would be strong communication abilities. Several weeks later when the Board of Education inserted its advertisement announcing the superintendent vacancy in the *Crusader* and other metropolitan newspapers and professional association journals, the leading requirement was "proven communication skills."

Among those who saw the vacancy announcement was Maria Alessi, a longtime principal and central office administrator in another part of the state. Maria's expertise was in areas of school budgets and curriculum development. She also possessed personal qualities that included a genuine fondness for people, a strong work ethic, and a sense of humor. Although she did not see herself as a person with strong communication skills, she decided to apply for the position as head of Carville schools. Shortly after mailing her application, Maria received a phone call from the Carville board secretary inviting her to come for an interview with the Board of Education.

QUESTIONS

1. Review Zachary Worthington's record as superintendent. Was the Board of Education wise in its decision to deny renewal of this contract? Explain.
2. What are some suggestions for Maria to consider as she prepares for her interview?
3. How important are communications skills as a prerequisite qualification for superintendent?
4. What are some specific strategies that Maria can offer to the Board of Education to demonstrate her communication abilities?

COMMENTS

Maria's campaign for superintendent does not begin with the phone call inviting her to interview, nor does it begin with her application. Like all upwardly mobile school leaders, Maria is building her skill set and experiences early on in her career. How can she do this? She needs to be involved in national and state professional associations and, if possible, assume a leadership role in these groups. She should attend professional conferences both to enhance her visibility and to increase her own growth as a school administrator. She should also make presentations on professional topics at conference seminars and workshops. She should read widely from professional journals and magazines. *The School Administrator*, the professional journal of the American Association of School Administrators, and *Educational Leadership*, a publication of the Association for Supervision and Curriculum Development, are recommended reading for those interested in central office leadership.

Maria should also develop her own network of advisers or mentors who can guide her in her career aspirations. She should initiate and expand gradually an issues file of significant concerns in education. She should also compile a portfolio of her professional career, making sure to include her own record of achievement, newspaper clippings, and letters of recognition.

Upon returning the phone call to interview, Maria's must move her campaign into high gear. She must download from the Internet the Carville school district report card and those for its individual schools. Information about school report cards is available from the web sites of state Boards of Education. Each Board of Education throughout the country has it own treasure trove of useful background information that can assist job applicants. Budget details for the schools and the district, mission statements, personnel listings, class size information, minutes of Board of Education meetings, pupil achievement data, and various policies and procedures can all be found on the web site of a school district. Maria needs to study this information in preparation for her interview.

Maria would be wise to visit the town of Carville. She can find useful nuggets of information from the local real estate office, the Chamber of Commerce, and the town library. She should read community brochures and any newsworthy materials that can augment her knowledge of Carville. She would do well to study the school district calendar and the vertical file in the library reference section. The latter file contains newspaper articles about local schools and is itself an extremely valuable source of information for serious job applicants. Armed with this background data, Maria is quite prepared for what is often the first question on an interview: "Tell us what you know about our school district."

Much of any effective leadership approach involves the ability to communicate with one's constituents. It may well be an administrator's most valuable asset. To be an effective communicator, Maria must develop trust. How? She must be honest, visible, and available; provide support; take a sincere interest in the lives of the people she serves; and respond to requests for information from the members of the Board of Education and the general public.

When she does not know an answer, Maria must say so: "I really don't have that information. Let me get back to you." And she better follow-up and get back with a response. Otherwise, she loses points on the trust scale. The expression is true that it takes five years to build a reputation and five minutes to lose it.

Maria can also adopt more structured approaches to strengthen lines of communication in the Carville community. As part of her leadership style she should require staff members to return all phone calls within twenty-four hours, but preferably the same day. This technique is as much a communication strategy as it is a management tool. Maria should assign a staff member to keep up to date with the Carville school district web site. She needs to plan for a regular district-wide newsletter. She may also want to contribute a column to the local newspaper. Does Carville participate in a local or regional broadcasting network? If so, volunteer to serve as a frequent guest. She might also speak at local civic or business meetings. When doing so, bring handouts and come with a PowerPoint presentation or a video of school events. Maria might also want to invite a student to accompany her—and speak at the meeting. Has any school employee performed exceptionally well? Invite that person.

Maria should also direct a staff member to write regular press releases for the *Carville Crusader*. She should also develop a relationship with the education reporter and invite that reporter to cover school events. And when community members volunteer their time in the schools, a note of thanks or an annual recognition luncheon would surely improve communication. In some school districts, depending on size, the superintendent personally sends birthday greetings.

Keeping the community aware of school activities is an increasingly important goal of school administrators. Community members want to feel a part of their schools. With good communication they will vote to support these schools too.

Chapter Five

Good Communication Is Essential

Distractions and poor communication limit the effectiveness of educators to maximize their efforts for the students. Today's schools are complex institutions that have a crucial responsibility for educating our youth. If the teachers complain that they are informed of program changes at the last possible moment, one has to believe there may be concerns about timely communication.

If the teachers are overwhelmed with memos, e-mails, faxes, and notices from the principal and central office, it becomes obvious that too many mandates and dictates can reduce the morale of the school's staff.

During a faculty meeting at the Madison School, Principal Joe Wilson listed "Faculty Concerns" on his agenda. After a few moments of silence, fourth-grade teacher Amy Adams spoke up and shocked the audience. Normally Amy is quiet and soft spoken. But today she was vocal and forthright. "With all due respect, I have to say that I'm fed up with all the notices giving us more and more responsibilities and especially paperwork to do." Well, that started quite a catharsis of distress.

"And don't forget about all the recordkeeping that you give us, Mr. Wilson," chimed in Tina Colon. John Howard, a fifth-grade teacher, called out, "How about the last minute notices of program changes?" Principal Wilson began to sense that something was going awry in his usually calm and ultra-cooperative staff. "And those intercom interruptions must stop. Many times I get a call from the office for a student in the midst of teaching. It annoys the students just when they are attentive and showing signs of learning," added second-grade teacher Aisha Johnson.

"What about the paperwork? We can't forget the monumental paperwork we have to do for the special programs for the central office and the state," shared Selma Rodder, a veteran reading teacher. Lastly, Robert Brown, a special ed teacher, voiced his comment. "When we get notices that an item analysis of an exam or a supply list or report cards are due to the administrator that same day for review, it is terribly overwhelming."

At the end of the faculty conference, Joe made some notes and was slightly shaking as he slowly walked toward his office. "Something has to be done to improve communications," he thought. He immediately called in his secretary and asked her about the intercom calls. She said that when parents come in requesting to take their children to the doctor she calls for the children quickly. "Those parents are impatient and so I comply to get them off my back," commented Secretary Ann Harris.

Principal Wilson decided to call a meeting of the outspoken teachers and the secretary to discuss improvements. It seemed to him that the criticisms were important to hear and even more important to correct. He planned the meeting for the next morning before school and each invitee agreed to come to the building early.

He spent that evening thinking about the boisterous faculty meeting. On one hand he thought that it was good for the staff to bring their concerns out into the open for airing and sharing. He desired to improve the school, which he loved working in for the past five years. He was going to take action quickly and vigorously not only to show the staff that he wished to cooperate and help them, but also to deal with what now seems to be a real concern to a staff he respected.

For a moment, he was upset that he had no inkling of these problems. Briefly he felt uncomfortable because he should have been aware of these issues just as he always prided himself on thinking that he knew what was going on at all times in his building. Another thought came to his mind. He was surprised that there was such anger about the communication in the building.

When he awoke in the morning he told himself he would use this situation to make the school a better place. He knew he was human and no one is perfect but at least he could work toward making the school a more comfortable place for all.

As the invited group entered his office, he had his notepad ready to take down the information and to request solutions for the problems presented yesterday.

Amy Adams began to speak and said, "Mr. Wilson, we know you want to do your best here and we have always admired you and respected you since you first began working here. But this issue of communication has been getting worse and bothering us terribly. When you gave us the opportunity to share our concerns, I just burst out hoping that you would listen and help us."

The others nodded their heads. Principal Wilson now felt confident that they could work together to come up with acceptable solutions.

QUESTIONS

1. Considering the outbursts, was it wise for Principal Wilson to include "Faculty Concerns" in the agenda?
2. Evaluate Principal Wilson's reaction to the criticism.
3. What are the possible solutions with regard to communication problems?

COMMENTS

Although Principal Wilson should be commended for his willingness to provide opportunities for the staff to vent and share feelings, perhaps he should have already known about the frustrations of the staff.

He may have gotten this information from those in the building whom he is close with. Often there are teachers or other administrators or office personnel who can inform the principal that the teachers seem quite upset about specific practices. These individuals need not be considered "snitches." Instead they can enlighten the principal about important circumstances that arise that truly require his understanding and knowledge.

His secretary, for example, may have heard something from teachers talking in the office. He may have been able to hear of the unhappiness when he met with individuals or small groups of teachers at various meetings in his office. He might have picked up signs of problems as he toured the building and made small talk with teachers.

Regardless of this inability to know about the need for better communication, he did take an excellent route to gain teacher input by including the agenda item and allowing them to speak up. He appears to be willing to work with the staff to improve morale. It was a superb professional decision to include the item about staff concerns in the faculty agenda.

The result could benefit the school if the committee and the principal work together to come up with realistic and relevant ways to improve communication. Of course, the resulting solutions will have to be implemented and evaluated after a time.

Principal Wilson reacted professionally to the criticism. He took immediate action to rectify the obvious problems by calling a meeting the next morning. He clearly showed the staff that he meant to do whatever it would take to clear up the unpleasant perceptions that appear to be prevalent in his school.

It is normal that he may have felt a little uncomfortable about not knowing what was going on; but, more importantly, he overcame that rapidly and was determined to see to it that he worked with the staff to remedy the situation.

Among the most common communication problems in schools are intercom announcements, last minute program changes without clear and timely notice, and paperwork reminders that interfere with the instructional process. In addition, numerous memos are a concern.

Unnecessary recordkeeping and paperwork requirements stress the staff. Often administrators add to the load that the central office and the state have mandated in an attempt to gather the statistics for monitoring students, especially those who are the weakest academically or the most troublesome behaviorally.

Unfunded mandates make educators furious because they are asked to take on or start a program without the proper monetary funding to provide the materials or sometimes adequate staff.

Good communication is essential for a well-managed school. At this morning meeting the immediate concerns of the staff could be taken up and perhaps a committee could be organized to meet with the principal on an ongoing basis. The committee could set up policies and procedures that could investigate all communication in the school and see where this could be clarified and where paperwork and recordkeeping could be refined or reduced or perhaps even eliminated.

Among the issues that could be taken up are the ones mentioned by the teachers at the meeting, which would further prompt a review of all communications.

There are several practices that would be beneficial. It is a good practice to issue a memo on Fridays so that the teachers have an idea of what is going to occur the following week. When the teachers come into school in the morning there should be a memo or daily notice posted on a board of some sort to tell them what is happening that day: who is going on a trip, whose class will be covered by whom, and whether there are any special meetings at lunchtime or some other time of the day. Also posted should be opportunities for workshops or meetings where teachers may sign up for training or enlightenment in an area of interest. As much as is possible information should be shared well in advance for the staff to plan for any changes.

As for the intercom announcements, the principal can speak at a parents' association meeting explaining that if the school is notified in advance, the teacher can see to it that the child is in the office when the parent arrives. If the parent calls the school in the morning of a last minute doctor's appointment, the teacher can be notified at lunchtime for an afternoon early dismissal of the child. The child, too, could be notified at lunch, avoiding the need to interrupt the entire class later on.

Brainstorming with the staff at a faculty meeting could deal with specific types of interruptions unique to the school. If the staff has computers in each room and there is no emergency, use e-mails to communicate. This is one way to communicate with the teachers about information that must be conveyed during the instructional program.

In some cases, the school may decide to even utilize texting to convey information to a teacher. This is a quiet and quick manner to communicate with the teacher and not disturb the students in the room. However, the office staff and the administration and all out of the classroom staff should never overwhelm the teachers with contacts during teaching time.

A monthly calendar for the parents should be made available to the staff so they too can understand what is going to happen. Communication with parents should also be via a web site and e-mails so they know about trips, test dates, and special assembly programs. The newsletters can be written in several languages if there are groups of non-English speakers in the school.

As for the paperwork, a committee of teachers can study all the paperwork and make suggestions as to what is annoying them the most. The principal and other administrators can take a close look at their recommendations and reduce or eliminate the paperwork that truly is not necessary for reports for the central office or for vital monitoring of the students.

Related to effective communication is creating minutes of meetings with decisions taken so that those in attendance have a record and those staff members not in attendance understand what happened and what plans were made.

Encouraging the central office or the state or even federal government to reduce paperwork and unfunded mandates is indeed a challenging task, to say the least. But, there are positive actions that a school staff can attempt. When politicians come to the school for special programs or to speak to parent groups, why not use the opportunity to respectfully inform them what concerns exist about state and federal government burdens? When the administrators go to the central office for meetings, they can voice their objections to unnecessary paperwork, programs, or policies.

Parents can be helpful if they are clearly aware of the problems that exist. If the parents' association president gets an opportunity to meet with central office personnel, he or she can espouse the cause of the school staff. Even the teachers' union chairperson can be vocal with politicians and central office personnel when given the chance to voice an opinion. Of course, at all times it is important to be polite, accurate, and calm and coherent when speaking and to avoid disparaging remarks.

Chapter Six

A Betrayal of Trust?

"Mr. Moore was my homeroom teacher. He kept touching me. When I asked him to stop, he said it was normal. I shouldn't be afraid. Later he was transferred to another school and everyone said it was my fault."

Fourteen-year-old Vicki Fletcher trusted Dan Moore. When she broke her leg he called her at home to inquire about her recuperation. He was the coach of the Harding School tennis team Vicki played for. And whenever she felt anxious about herself as a maturing teenage girl, Dan Moore spoke to her like her father. Mr. Moore lent a sympathetic ear. In some ways, he had replaced her father who had died a short time ago in a car accident. Her dad's untimely death was a difficult ordeal for the entire family and for Vicki in particular. Dan's presence in her life had begun to fill the void left by her father's absence.

Dan was a highly regarded science teacher who volunteered many hours to serve students as a tennis coach, as a tutor for those in danger of failing, and as a mentor for those students who needed extra support during their turbulent teen years. The entire community respected Dan for his pleasant demeanor, good teaching skills, and his willingness to help his students in any way they needed—until the allegations of abuse. Vicki's mother demanded of the school board an official investigation of the charges against her daughter's teacher.

The Board of Education members peppered Superintendent Randy Tomlinson with numerous questions: How long had they known each other? Where did this incident take place? Were other students unwitting victims of this abuse? Had Dan Moore ever been disciplined before for this or other indiscretions? With what results? Were other employees aware of this incident or other similar incidents? What mechanisms were in place to prevent sexual abuse against students by faculty and staff? Did anyone report any such suspicions to school authorities? What is the liability of the Board of Education in this matter? How can the board resolve this dilemma without protracted litigation? What support can the school district give to Vicki and the other students at Harding?

Randy Tomlinson immediately grasped the seriousness of the situation and conducted a thorough investigation with the help of board attorney Sam Johnston, the district director of guidance June Handelman, and school principal Ron Shakespeare. On that particular day, Vicki asked Dan if he had time to assist her in preparation for an upcoming science fair project. "Of course, Vicki, you know I am always here for you. Let's meet during lunch in my science lab," exclaimed Dan. "I'll put you on the right track."

After Dan allegedly exploited Vicki, she was visibly shaken and in tears. She confided to her best friend Megan Martin who ran to tell the principal. Disbelieving of the allegation against such a popular teacher, Ron queried Dan who dismissed it as a case of a troubled girl who came on to him. "I was going to tell you after school, Ron, but I guess Vicki beat me to it. She is setting me up," added Dan.

The investigation revealed that Vicki's own credibility was tenuous at best. She had been disciplined in the past by her teachers for lying about an extended three-day absence from school. Claiming she was attending an out-of-town funeral for her uncle, Vicki was really at home playing hooky with friends who attended another school. Upon her return to school, Vicki forged her mother's signature on the absence note.

Weighing the credibility of each and the circumstances, Ron did not pursue the matter and intended to close his internal review due to Ron's impeccable record and Vicki's own history of taking liberties with the truth. Eager to protect Vicki's privacy and unwilling to tarnish the reputation of a respected teacher, Ron did not report the matter to the superintendent because no policy existed that required administrators to report suspicion of sexual misconduct by a staff member against a student.

Elaine Fletcher thought otherwise and pressured the Board of Education to establish a policy to prevent future occurrences. Angry board members agreed and directed superintendent Randy to draft a policy to address such situations.

QUESTIONS

1. Evaluate Dan Moore's behavior and actions in this case.
2. Evaluate principal Ron Shakespeare's behavior and actions in this case.
3. What advice would you offer Randy as he works to design a policy on sexual harassment?

COMMENTS

As caring as he was about the progress of his students, Dan compromised his own integrity by meeting with Vicki privately in the science lab. In doing so he may have set himself up to be the target of a complaint. In the current climate Dan would be wise never to work alone with a student but to work with a group of youngsters. He should have sought a more public place and left the door open to avoid these kinds of accusations and recriminations.

In the absence of a policy mandating a report, school principal Ron Shakespeare may be legally correct in not reporting the incident to the superintendent's office. However, as the ultimate child advocate, he would have been advised to do so. Depending on state statutes, policies, and the collective bargaining agreement, the superintendent may order an administrative transfer for Dan or put him on paid leave pending resolution of the complaint.

Sexual misconduct results in an unsafe environment for teachers and students. Children who are victims often develop low self-esteem and patterns of excessive absence. The potential for lawsuits also heightens the responsibility of a Board of Education to create a policy. Courts have ruled that students may sue and collect damages from school districts whose employees abuse students.

It is incumbent on the superintendent and the Board of Education to create a policy. Shoop (2003) outlines a number of provisions that could be included in the policy:

1. a statement that sexual misconduct will not be tolerated;
2. a description of specific behaviors that are inappropriate;
3. a requirement that all staff members, including teachers, office aides, and cafeteria workers, report all allegations by students;
4. clear guidelines to faculty that limit closed door, private encounters with students;
5. a signed statement from each school employee that he or she had received the policy and has read it;
6. comprehensive training on an annual basis for all Board of Education employees;
7. screening of potential employees, including fingerprinting, to determine if they have ever been convicted of sexual misconduct;
8. background checks with previous employers to determine potential employee involvement in matters of exploitation against minors;
9. upgrading of school handbooks to clearly delineate the policy;
10. a centralized monitoring system that tracks complaints against staff members and the disposition of complaints;

11. appointment of one specific coordinator on the school and district levels to record and resolve incidents of exploitation;
12. creation of a mobile team of trained counselors to assist students who report, or may be the victims of, incidents of abuse;
13. dissemination to parents of the policy;
14. procedures for reporting and investigation of complaints.

Several professional and private organizations offer resources on sexual abuse issues. The National Education Association (NEA) has published a sexual exploitation manual titled *Flirting or Hurting? A Teacher's Guide to Student Sexual Harassment in Schools*. NEA has also distributed educational materials and held workshops to raise awareness of this issue. The National Association of State Boards of Education offers a document titled "Sexual Harassment in Schools: A Policy Guide" that includes recommendations, a sample policy, a student guide for understanding sexual harassment at school, and teachings strategies on the topic.

REFERENCE

Shoop, R. J. 2003. *Sexual exploitation: How to spot it and stop it.* Thousand Oaks, CA: Corwin Press.

Chapter Seven

The Principal as the Instructional Leader: Part 1

The Main Street School was an ideal place for a principal to work. The parents were supportive. The students for the most part were serious and well behaved. The teachers were experienced and dedicated. One of the few problems the school had was that the population was changing and the reading scores were declining. Because of the superb reputation of the school, parents from poorer areas wanted to move into that community to be able to give their children a better education. Immigrant families heard of the reputation through foreign language newspapers that wrote laudatory articles about the school. Families that had been struggling to survive economically heard from neighbors and relatives that the Main Street School treated children with respect, had high expectations, and even youngsters with problems made exemplary progress in the academic subjects.

The former principal, Arnold Hairston, was well respected. He had worked at the school for fifteen years. He was a kind, caring, and pensive person. He enjoyed chatting with parents and teachers. He spent much time listening to the concerns of the secretaries, school aides, and teacher assistants. Arnold often took time to listen to the children read. The pupils in the school felt comfortable walking over to him and talking about whatever was on their minds. Arnold was a real people person. But, with the demographics of the school changing, Arnold, at age sixty-two, realized that the school he loved so much needed a new type of principal. He realized that the reading scores were going down because a large number of the incoming students were far below average in reading. For two years prior to his retirement three-fourths of the incoming students were well below average. So he decided to retire.

At the end of the interviewing process, the selection committee agreed that Frank Conway should be selected as the new principal. Frank had been an assistant principal who possessed a strong curriculum background. He was experienced in staff training and was thoroughly familiar with new programs the school would have to utilize if it was to continue to be an outstanding educational institution.

The first thing Frank did was to meet in small groups with the teachers to review their strengths and weaknesses. He also learned what they enjoyed teaching the most. He met with the secretarial staff to hear about their experiences and to let them know what he expected. He met with the teacher aides and other employee groups to learn what their responsibilities were. Frank attended parents' association meetings to answer questions, and he informed the general population about his background and what he hoped to do for the school. He sat in on parent executive board meetings when he was invited to explain his goals for the school.

During the second month at the Main Street School, Frank organized a curriculum committee. This committee consisted of four teachers. One represented the upper grades. One represented the lower grades. One represented the out-of-classroom, specialist teachers. The fourth person was the faculty chairperson. At the meeting everyone agreed that changes needed to be made in the instructional program. Frank realized that the staff was made up of veteran teachers. The teacher experience level averaged more than ten years. He decided that he was going to upgrade their skills by bringing in a new series of books. He would start with reading and then math. After that Frank would concentrate on social studies and finally science. He told the committee that the teachers should select the series since they would be using the books. The only criteria he insisted on was that the reading series should be in line with the balanced reading approach, that all teachers must use the series, and that it should relate to curriculum standards as well as the tests the students would be taking. He suggested that they contact nearby schools and inquire if they were all using the same materials or if there was one that the majority used. He indicated they should seek to get the publishers to demonstrate their series to the staff.

Once the textbooks had been purchased, Frank asked the publisher's sales representative to send in consultants to explain the use of the materials. Frank knew he could not directly tell the veteran teachers they needed to upgrade their skills. Instead, he told the consultant to weave the new methods and techniques into her discussion about how to use the textbooks. He then set up bimonthly meetings for the consultant to meet with each grade level's teachers to review the materials as well as to give them a chance to ask questions that would be geared to helping each teacher with his or her specific class. In addition, Frank met monthly with the teachers of each grade to review the concerns they had. Frank also visited all the classes daily and he gave the teachers feedback on what he observed. If the feedback was to be negative or critical, he met with the teacher individually.

During a faculty conference in his fourth month as the principal, several teachers brought up the need for a definitive discipline policy. Frank organized a group of teachers to meet and develop a policy that comprised common infractions and appropriate interventions when necessary. He consulted with the student council and reviewed the policy with the parents' association president prior to implementing it as a school-wide policy. The policy seemed to be what was needed and proved to be effective.

QUESTIONS

1. How could Frank handle the low reading scores that came about because of the large numbers of students entering the school with low reading scores?
2. What are some measures he could take to avoid major discipline problems in the school?
3. In addition to strengthening the reading and discipline plans, what else could Frank do to maintain the school as an excellent place to attend?

COMMENTS

Regardless of the superb nature of the staff and the materials and the total commitment of everyone in the school, when a large number of pupils enter with significantly poor reading scores, it is a challenge to raise those scores. The best that can be done is to work with fervor, skill, and dedication to keep the decline minimal. Often students who come to a school and are several years behind cannot all be helped to score on level in one or even two years.

Some may make fantastic progress, but a large number cannot improve three or more years under normal, honest circumstances. The principal and the staff need to communicate with the parents, the central headquarters, and the community at large and let them know what is occurring and hope that they understand the changes taking place. When youngsters enter the school the reading teacher or some other person knowledgeable about testing should give the new pupils a reading test. The records from the former school should be checked to see what level the student was performing at in the previous school. Statistics need to be compiled to show that many youngsters are entering the school below level. A course of action needs to be developed by the staff and the central office. The parents should be told of the plans to be undertaken to make changes for the new population.

There are a number of things a principal could undertake to avoid major discipline problems. Effective instruction is a significant way to avoid discipline problems. Students who are learning and enjoying it usually do not cause discipline problems. In addition, the staff needs to display to the pupils a firm personality. When the staff members clearly illustrate that they are determined and confident for the youngsters to behave well, it usually limits discipline problems. The *power of personality* is the very best way to avoid or decrease discipline problems. Other means for avoiding discipline problems are to develop a realistic code of behavior and adhere to it. Another way to limit or avoid discipline problems is for the staff to take time to talk to those who could cause the problems. Included in this group are students who are far below in the academic area, students whose parents may be going through a divorce, and students who have emotional problems. Talking to them on a regular basis can go a long way toward helping them to adjust. Listening to them tell what is upsetting them is essential. Having them write down what is occurring and why "others" bother them is vital. Workshops for parents in large or small groups with staff members enable the parents to work along with the school. The parents can voice their concerns and opinions and the staff can get a sense of what parents are thinking. This could be helpful in organizing a discipline program. Individual parent conferences can also be helpful. Perhaps a plan can be set up at these meetings for the parents to take some responsibility with regard to their children's discipline needs. When parents are not helpful, the school needs to set up in-house measures to involve the parents. Lastly, involving the psychologist, social worker, and guidance counselor and other ancillary staff can be of valuable assistance.

Frank should set up end-of-the-year activities such as field days, concerts, and art exhibits. The specialist teachers in each of these areas could begin working early in the year toward the culminating activity, and the students could prepare and have an opportunity to excel. Students who are not the best in academics could be fully involved as well as the brighter youngsters. All students then have a chance to be stars. Every specialist teacher should be requested to have an end of year activity in which all their students have a chance to display their talents.

Chapter Eight

The Principal as the Instructional Leader: Part 2

The Webster School was not the most pleasant place to work in. Quite a few youngsters were rowdy and undisciplined. Teachers were demoralized and tired. The parents could be vocal and often very angry. The one bright spot in the school was the physical education program. Every student loved going to the gym. The exercise program was healthy. The instructional portion was relevant to the game they would be playing that day, and the games were always great fun.

When students walked into the gym they immediately behaved like model citizens. For some reason James Carmichael, the teacher, possessed such stature and reputation that no one dared to misbehave in the gym or in the field when he was present. The parents had enormous respect for him. The teachers were delighted when their students came back to their rooms from the physical education class because the students were calm and motivated to learn. James Carmichael indeed was someone everyone admired.

When the principal's job was vacant after the former principal retired because of a serious illness, the staff and the parents and even the students petitioned the superintendent to appoint James Carmichael as the principal. James had been an administrative assistant in order to obtain his state supervision and administrative certificate. James was the person everyone turned to because of the strong disciplinarian he was.

Few applicants applied for the principalship of this challenging school, and James won out over the other candidates after the selection process ended. James was called in to the superintendent's office just prior to beginning his new assignment. "You are popular and you are known to be fair and caring. You've been a big help to the teachers and the youngsters respect and like you. But you will have two major problems as principal. I can help you and so will my staff. But you will have to do much on your own," Superintendent Betsy Walker told him.

"What will be my biggest problems?" James questioned.

"You may have to get firm with some teachers who have been your longtime friends. And, the even bigger problem is that the reading scores in this school are abysmal. You have no in-depth background to tackle that. I can help you with that through the district's reading coordinator. You can also consult with the reading coach in your school. You have a monumental task in front of you," added Superintendent Walker.

James did not sleep that night.

The next day he called a meeting after school. He frankly told the staff of his two problems. He said, "you all know I have been your friend for many, many years, seventeen in all. If I have to correct something I see or if I have complaints about what a parent or child reveals to me, how do you want me to handle it?" The staff appreciated his frankness and willingness to be open and candid right from the start. They shared several helpful ideas. Basically they told him not to be afraid to criticize; just be sure it is fair and do it in private. They said he should come with specific suggestions on how to improve.

Then James said he had one more issue to address. "We have a major reading weakness at the Webster School. I want to resolve it and get the reading scores much higher. I need your help to do that. You know I am not a reading expert and as a matter of fact I have very little experience with the teaching or understanding of the skill of teaching reading." Again, the teachers were willing to do their share. They suggested that the reading coach be his close adviser on this issue. They also said they should have regular meetings to talk about what they were doing and what they thought needed to be done to improve the school's reading scores and suggested what role he could play even with his limited experience in this area.

The very next day James met with the reading coach, Clarice Johnson. She had two major recommendations. Clarice said, "The first thing we have to do is to make sure that we have a balanced and effective reading program. We can review the school-wide program and each teacher's reading techniques over a period of time and make changes as needed. The second is that we must have a comprehensive test preparation program that helps the students to become familiar with the format of the tests."

With Clarice's help, James visited the classes each day and tried to get there when reading was being taught. Clarice suggested that he go with her to local reading conferences and talk to salesmen about reading materials, storybooks, and test preparation materials. Clarice and James met with all the teachers at least once a month in small groups and large ones. Sometimes they met with individuals to go over specific assistance that could be provided for their classes or to listen to the teachers explain what progress or lack of progress occurred. Clarice showed James how to review the work and practice tests that children completed. Clarice said she would lead conferences on new ideas in reading research for the staff. She added that James must be there or she would not do it. Clarice also informed James of the ethics involved in test preparation and testing in general. She gave him guidelines that he incorporated into a memo, and he reviewed it at a faculty conference.

Within a few years the reading scores began to improve. James was proud of how he had encouraged the staff to assist him to make the gains in the reading. "Now that reading is going in the right direction, I'll add math and then science and then social studies as goals in the coming years," he told the staff.

QUESTIONS

1. What do you think of the way James handled his particular situation considering his limited background?
2. What more could be done to help the reading scores in this school?
3. What other resources could James utilize to help the school improve?
4. What could he be sacrificing by placing an extraordinary emphasis on the reading program?

COMMENTS

James was quite right to go to the staff for assistance and to incorporate their ideas into his decision-making process. Using the reading coach to help him in an area he honestly stated was unknown to him was brave and astute. He made the staff take ownership of the improvement process by involving them from the beginning. He strengthened his own position by working closely with the staff and showing them that he respected them.

James could utilize the reading coordinator from the central office to help him understand the superintendent's reading goals as well as to find out what has been working well in the other schools. James could also have his teachers make presentations at the parents' association meetings to help them understand the changes that were taking place in the reading program. He could read journals and other reading-related magazines and distribute interesting articles to teachers in their mailboxes on Friday afternoons. He could ask teachers who were teaching interesting and exciting lessons to speak to the other teachers at meetings. He could advocate intervisitations and common planning.

Anytime a principal places great stress on one aspect of the educational program other sectors suffer. Perhaps the arts program or the music program or physical education may suffer. Sometimes the library and the science and social studies programs suffer. Teachers quickly notice when the administration wants the reading scores to go up, and they spend less time teaching social studies and science or incorporating the arts into the daily schedule. Parents who want a full physical education program sometimes get upset when reading is overly stressed. Sometimes trips suffer when there is a tremendous emphasis on reading. It is difficult to balance the enormous effort it takes to improve reading in a school with the need to provide a broad and balanced education for all the students.

Chapter Nine

"We Are Normal Too"

Jimmy Jansen and Willie Larkin were an inseparable duo. Every morning they could be seen coming to school together. At lunch they often sat together. During recess they often chatted with each other and rarely participated in the usual banter of their classmates. At dismissal they sought each other out as they made their way to one of the many extracurricular after school programs offered at the Red Creek High School. Chess was their favorite club activity, and they often competed against each other.

Few classmates or staff noticed the intense closeness between Jimmy and Willie. They lived near each other in the same town and belonged to the same church. It was not until they were seen kissing and holding hands in the school library that the nature of their friendship became public.

When news of their relationship began to circulate, the reaction was swift and not pleasant. Mary Lou Hynes, principal at Red Creek High School, responded quickly to the phone calls, letters, and e-mails she received from parents. In meeting with Jimmy and Willie, she found that they were indeed attracted to each other and had begun to express their mutual affection by holding hands. "This is who we are, and our parents are comfortable too. We hope you accept us as well." They added they had no intention of refraining from public displays of affection. Jimmy also informed the principal he would take Willie as his date to the upcoming senior prom.

A few days later, Mary Lou received a phone call from Jerry and Cindy Hudson whose son and daughter both attended Red Creek. They expressed quite vehemently to Mary Lou that unless she took action against those "faggots," they would lead a parent boycott of the school. They had already collected over one hundred signatures on a petition condemning this "abomination" and school officials for "condoning this mockery of our religious heritage." Students had begun to collect their own petitions urging Mary Lou to cancel the prom if Jimmy and Willie were going to be allowed to attend.

Fearful that some groups would carry out their threat and wishing to avoid negative publicity, Mary Lou again met with Jimmy and Willie and their parents. She conveyed to the boys and their parents public displays of affection and their intention to attend the prom as a couple were disruptive to the learning process and subjected them to possible harm from classmates. She urged the parents to "speak sense" to their sons and help them understand the danger they courted by their actions. Mary Lou asked them to just wait until after graduation "a couple of months away" before they resumed their relationship.

Jimmy, Willie, and their parents were not deterred by Mary Lou's recommendations. Later that evening, she received an e-mail that the families regarded Mary Lou's comments as a "veiled threat that infringes on Jimmy and Willie's First Amendment rights of free speech." The following day both boys again spoke with their principal. They informed her that since graduation was a short time away, they wished to form a Day of Diversity when students would organize class activities around issues such as race, class, gender, identity, and sexual orientation. "We want to educate the other students so they understand we are normal too and have feelings," interjected Willie. They added another request to organize a Day of Silence during which students would remain quiet for an entire day to raise awareness on behalf of gay, lesbian, bisexual, and transgender students. Finally, they stated it was their intention to form a Gay-Straight Alliance as a student club activity.

A shaken principal again explained graduation activities were a couple of months away and perhaps they would postpone their plans pending further study. "You're right, Ms. Hynes, graduation is a couple of months away. We have to organize soon."

QUESTIONS

1. Would you consider Mary Lou's comments a "veiled threat"?
2. What are Mary Lou's responsibilities under the law?
3. How should Mary Lou respond to the concerns of Jerry and Cindy Hudson?
4. Should Mary Lou allow Jimmy and Willie to attend the prom as a couple?

COMMENTS

One should not view Mary Lou's remarks to Jimmy and Willie's parents as a veiled threat. More likely, her well-intentioned remarks were designed to promote appropriate safety in a proper learning environment. This is a reasonable goal of any administrator. Nonetheless, it is a well-established principle of educational law that students do not leave their rights at the front door of the school. Mary Lou's zeal for order and safety cannot be allowed to thwart or restrict Jimmy's and Willie's rights under the First Amendment.

This scenario highlights a number of legal issues. Do Jimmy and Willie have the legal right to engage in acts of public affection during school hours? Can school officials deny them the right to attend the prom as a couple? When students wish to form a Gay-Straight Alliance, what is the school's obligation? Can the school legally deny the students' request to hold a Diversity Day and Day of Silence?

As Mary Lou begins to devise a plan to resolve the legal thicket she is immersed in, her first step would be to alert her superiors to the brewing controversy. She will need to maintain contact with the superintendent, board attorney, and the public relations unit at the superintendent's office.

As gay students eager to express their mutual affection, Jimmy and Willie are afforded the equal protection rights under the Fourteenth Amendment and free speech and association rights under the First Amendment. These rights apply to gay, lesbian, bisexual, and transgender (GLBT) students. Like other student clubs, GLBT-related student groups must be given equal protection and access under the Equal Access Act of 1984. Some courts have also ruled that Title IX of the Education Amendments of 1972 prohibits gender-based discrimination in educational programs that receive federal funds.

In Mary Lou's efforts to address the issues raised by Jerry and Cindy Hudson, the board attorney would certainly advise her that under the Equal Access Act, schools may not deny equal access to, or discriminate against, any group of students who may seek to conduct a meeting on the basis of religious, political, philosophical, or other content of the speech. A school may not deny a group like the Gay-Straight Alliance to meet because other parents, teachers, students, community members, or other administrators may protest. Justification for limiting free speech cannot be based on the relative popularity, or lack thereof, of a club's views. Unpopularity of views is no reason to deny student speech as noted in a 1969 landmark student rights case (*Tinker v. Des Moines Independent Community School District*, 393 U.S. 503, 508–509).

Where activists like the Hudsons may seek to disrupt the rights of Jimmy and Willie, school administrators must address them. Although the Equal Access Act allows schools to maintain order and discipline on school premises and to protect the well-being of students against threatening forces, courts have determined that school districts may not use this provision of the law to exclude GLBT clubs because of angry sentiment by hostile community members.

The courts would also uphold Jimmy and Willie in their desire to go to the prom as a couple on grounds that schools may not unfairly deny one's gender expression. In this case responsible school leaders like Mary Lou must devise a plan that protects their rights while simultaneously providing a safe environment for all. A threat by any group of students to boycott the prom if Jimmie and Willie attend is insufficient reason to cancel the event. The principle of *Tinker* is applicable to this situation.

A school's legal rights and responsibilities to sponsor events like a Day of Diversity and a Day of Silence depends on whether the activity is sponsored by the school or students. Schools generally exercise less control over student-initiated events than over the school's own events. When reviewing requests to hold such events, the school must be mindful of student rights. Although the First Amendment allows schools to limit speech that is lewd, indecent, or clearly offensive, requests by Jimmy and Willie to organize events like a Day of Diversity or a Day of Silence do not fall within the prohibitions of the amendment. Mary Lou should review the school policy that governs student-initiated events and apply the policy fairly to GLBT activities that are consistent with the law. Because the law is complex and subject to nuances of fact, situation, and jurisdiction, it is difficult to generalize. While some states, for example, may permit a Day of Diversity with few restrictions, others may impose a restriction to allow such events as long as they do not interfere with the educational mission of the school.

Because court rulings may differ in different states, Mary Lou must consult with legal counsel for her school district. It is always prudent for an administrator to seek legal advice to ascertain the specific legal response. To do otherwise and ignore judicial precedent may invite further legal challenge.

ADDITIONAL RESOURCES

The listing of these resources does not constitute an endorsement of the content or advice within these sites.

American Psychological Association. Just the Facts about Sexual Orientation and Youth: A Primer for Principals, Educators and School Personnel. Washington, D.C.: American Psychological Association. Retrieved from www.apa.org/pi/lgbc/publications/just_the_facts.aspx.

Council of School Attorneys. Resources, news, and court opinions on school law issues, including student rights. Available at www.nsba.org/cosa.

National Gay and Lesbian Task Force Policy Institute. Education Policy: Issues Affecting Gay, Lesbian, Bisexual and Transgender Youth. Available at www.thetaskforce.org/reports_and_research/education_policy.

Chapter Ten

The Elemiddle School

The debate at a recent Garrisonville Board of Education meeting was more passionate than the debates at other meetings. At issue at this particular session was a proposal to convert the district's elementary schools from K-5 configurations into K-8 designs. Superintendent Tanya Hanley and her staff had done their homework before the meeting in anticipation of a heated debate over the proposal.

Armed with statistics and research (Chaker, 2005) that she shared with the public in a very professional PowerPoint presentation, Tanya patiently laid out the case for K-8 schools:

- Preteen students do better academically in K-8 schools than their counterparts in middle schools with grades 6–8;
- Fewer disciplinary disruptions occur in K-8 schools than in middle schools;
- The trend in school construction is away from middle school design and in favor of K-8 designs: in the past ten years, there has been a 17 percent increase in the total number of K-8 schools in comparison with a 9 percent increase in the number of elementary schools;
- Middle school students have more negative attitudes about school than their K-8 peers;
- K-8 students have higher attendance than their peers in middle school.

Tanya then described the experiences of other school districts that had converted to K-8 designs. In particular, she described the positive success of other school districts around the country.

Here public speaking time began in earnest. Mary Steiner, a parent at the Water Mill School, thanked Tanya and the Board of Education members for their efforts over many months to bring the new design to this final stage of a public vote. She urged the board to approve the plan, adding that "as a parent I am happy knowing my four children will be under the same roof right up to high school. Kids grow up too fast today. This new idea gives parents like me the assurance the children will be safer and more protected." Several other parents and community members echoed Mary's remarks.

The debate began to heat up when John Barnwell came to the microphone. Long a gadfly at board meetings, John was unusually caustic in his criticism of the initiative to create a K-8 design. As a banker in the community, John cautioned Tanya and her team about the costs and financing of the plan. John was critical about other planning issues surrounding the idea such as building science labs, computer terminals, and additional library space to accommodate the more intense middle school course of study.

Others expressed similar misgivings about the plan. Some thought early adolescents did not belong in the same school environment with younger children who might be bullied. Others were concerned about teacher qualifications and whether child-oriented elementary school teachers could effectively teach a subject-oriented middle school curriculum.

After a long and vituperative debate, the Board of Education approved the superintendent's plan to convert the Garrisonville elementary schools into K-8 designs. The board directed Tanya to begin implementation of the plan. Before the end of the meeting, however, John Barnwell seized the microphone and shouted, "This fight's not over yet!"

QUESTIONS

1. What does the research tell about the effectiveness of K-8 models?
2. What other planning issues should Tanya consider as her team shifts to K-8 schools?
3. How should the board and the superintendent respond to the criticism leveled by John Barnwell?

COMMENTS

Long considered the stepchild of public education, middle schools have been blamed for increases in student misbehavior, alienation, and poor achievement. The enactment of the No Child Left Behind Act, with its heavy reliance on testing and accountability, has intensified some of these issues. As pupil academic achievement becomes the chief determinant of a school's success, educators are placing less emphasis on the social-emotional needs of preteens. Because achievement of young teens is often coupled with their developmental needs, a lack of attention to the emotional well-being of students compromises their academic performance levels.

Tanya's presentation at the Board of Education meeting was quite detailed in discussing the rationale for a change to K-8 schools. According to a RAND Corporation report (Juvonen et al. 2004), research concludes that the onset of teen puberty is an especially weak reason to begin a new phase in a child's education. The combination of changes in a child's maturation that occurs simultaneously with adjustment to the new configuration of middle school adds to the stress of children. Other studies note that students perform better in schools that emphasize both academics and personal attention.

Clearly Tanya's arguments to convert the schools to a K-8 configuration are educationally sound. Tanya provided proper leadership in this case and took into account the current research and best practices. Her decision appears to be guided by a philosophy based on the interests of students when she made her recommendation to the Board of Education.

Now Tanya must address the practical issues as she implements the plan. Among these are financing, conversion of classrooms to science labs, parents concerns about student safety, professional development of faculty, upper grade parent involvement, and more specialized technology equipment and space.

The new configuration will obviously require a price tag about which Tanya most assuredly has advised the Board of Education. An increase in state and local taxes plus perhaps the sale of long-term bonds will cover additional costs. Tanya must sell the community on the educational value of the K-8 design. Her team must secure bids as it hires a company with expertise in educational construction. Parent concerns about the safety of younger children mixing with upper grade youngsters can be addressed by considering separate entrances, separate lunchrooms, and different arrival and dismissal schedules.

A key policy concern about middle schools is that many teachers lack subject matter certification in the areas they teach. In addition, many have little awareness of the developmental needs of preadolescents. If her plan is to succeed, Tanya and her team must develop evidence-based models of professional development that will enhance faculty expertise in their subject areas and, at the same time, provide training in the unique social-emotional developmental issues of preadolescence.

Parent involvement in school activities often wanes as students proceed through their school careers. In many instances middle schools do not properly engage parents in their children's education. The result is a further decline in parent participation. Tanya must engage her staff in researching effective middle school models of parent involvement. Parents themselves should play a significant role in this effort.

While the planning team is addressing the substantive issues of implementing the policy of the Board of Education, Tanya must respond to the challenge posed by John Barnwell. John poses a threat due to the power he possesses. The source of this power, of course, is his vocal dissent and his expertise in banking. If he is not handled properly, his opposition could scuttle the plan.

Tanya would be wise to meet privately with John and listen carefully to his views. She must find ways to make him an ally or at least mute his vocal opposition. Some plausible strategies she might consider include inviting him to serve on the planning committee, using his financial expertise to identify funding sources, and encouraging him to participate in plans that visit sites where K-8 configurations are operating. Tanya must cultivate John as a potential ally rather than a caustic opponent. This will require honesty on her part, an open door policy toward John, and strong lines of communication between them.

REFERENCES

Chaker, A. M. 2005. Middle school goes out of fashion. *Wall Street Journal* April 6, pp. D1, D4.

Juvonen, J., V. Le, T. Kaganoff, C. Augustine, and L. Constant. 2004. *Focus on the wonder years: Challenges facing the American middle school.* Santa Monica, CA: RAND.

Chapter Eleven

A Community of Principals

Fortunately for Superintendent Vivian Blair, when she used inferences the principals at her conferences understood she had positive intentions. During one of the principal conferences she said, "I think it would be beneficial if the principals had lunch once a week. Choose a restaurant where at least four or five of you could meet and have lunch on Thursdays."

The amazed principals peered at one another with questioning stares. For years now, leaving the building other than for conferences was practically forbidden. So why had Vivian Blair made this statement?

On the following Thursday morning groups of four or five principals called one another and made plans to eat lunch at mutually convenient restaurants. Each informed the secretary and assistant where he or she would be and left with both an uneasy and yet a happy feeling.

It was quite pleasant to ask one another about spouses, children, and other personal questions. It was good to share what their own children were accomplishing in school. The conversation was enjoyable, and it was good to have a lunch free of interruptions of calls and no one asking to talk to the principal in the middle of lunch.

While the principals were having coffee and dessert, one principal, John Hall, revealed a problem he was having in his school. "I have a parent who is driving me crazy because the teacher will not take her child on the class trip next week."

"Why is that?" asked Sarah Cunningham.

"The boy ran away from the group two months ago on a trip to the museum and now the teacher fears that the boy will run from the tour at the zoo next week. The mother will not relent. She says that he must go with the class because he will feel left out and he might experience psychological trauma. She has called me several times, come to see me, and written long letters to the teacher."

Sarah Cunningham responded, "I had a problem like that two years ago and I told the teacher to tell the mother that the child could go on the trip if the mother attended and chaperoned the child. That solved the problem. That boy never ran away from the group ever again because the mother had to go on every trip until he graduated from the school.

"That's the answer," stated John Hall. His problem was solved.

Bill Armstrong asked the group a question: "I heard a rumor that teachers were upset because they put up fabulous bulletin boards and I did not send them notes thanking them for the wonderful bulletin boards which were relevant and had a high level of pupil participation."

Henry Sharp had a good suggestion for Bill. "I made up a form letter for activities like that where the teachers worked hard and contributed something marvelous. They want to feel they are appreciated for excellence. I made up a form letter and left room for individualizing the comments. In this way they get a thank you for going above and beyond for the school and the students and for me. I write one or two sentences that are specific to each one so that they feel that are not all getting the same letter. If you like I will fax you my form letter and you can adapt it as you wish."

When the lunch was over, John Hall was thinking to himself, "Now I see why Vivian wanted us to have lunch. So many problems can be solved by another principal who has experienced it before. This community of principals is marvelous for saving time and overcoming aggravation."

QUESTIONS

1. Why is this informal method of helping one another so reasonable and practical?
2. How else could John Hall have handled the problem child and trip attendance?
3. What are other ways that a community of principals can share experiences and help one another?

COMMENTS

When principals have lunch together they are relaxed and feel comfortable bringing up sensitive or complex dilemmas for discussion. It is effective because often other principals have faced similar problems and have the experience to respond with helpful answers. Even if the principal did not have a positive or favorable outcome, it could help the requesting principal because he or she can benefit from the experiences of the explaining principal.

The lunch atmosphere is informal and allows give and take in a manner that is positive for discussing. Sensitive issues can be discussed because colleagues do not rate or evaluate one another. Therefore, one can feel at ease to ask for advice and to receive it from those who know precisely what the speaker is asking about.

John could ask the school social worker or guidance counselor to meet with the child and see if counseling might help the youngster. He could also talk to the teacher to see if there is any remorse on the part of the child, and maybe the child has shown a real desire to do the right thing on the next trip. John could tell the child that he could go on the trip but would be severely punished by suspension or some other consequence if he ran away once again. On the other hand, John could back the teacher fully and not allow the child to go on the trip. This would send a message to all children and parents that youngsters must act responsibly or there will be serious consequences. This also sends a signal to the teachers that the principal backs them up and insists on correct behavior from the students at all times.

The superintendent could set up committees of principals to work on specific issues that relate to each of them. Central office staff specialists could meet with groups of principals and lead round table discussions with regard to common problems in curriculum. Perhaps the district specialists could meet with principals with regard to supervising teachers and documenting their performance when necessary. Principals could meet in their colleagues' schools for tours to see special programs that others may wish to adopt. Principals can invite others to observe teachers for set purposes and then meet to discuss what they observed. Principals can attend local and national conferences and set up plans to follow-up what the speakers suggested. Principals can meet on a regular basis to brainstorm specific topics of mutual interest.

Chapter Twelve

Ninety Percent of Success Is Showing Up

Principal Helen O'Brien of the Winston School received a note from an upset teacher, Barbara Wayne. Barbara informed Helen that a student named Mary had not arrived at school again. Mary was a child Helen was watching carefully because she was in the fourth grade but was functioning on the first-grade level and had an abysmal attendance record.

Mary had entered the school in September and immediately the principal was concerned because the evaluating reading teacher said that Mary was very far behind and had few reading skills. Mary was a lovely child. When she came to school, she behaved well and although she was quite deficient academically, she followed the directions of the teacher and seemed to try to be a good student. When doing actual school work, Mary put forth a satisfactory effort although the work was extremely frustrating for her. Helen felt Mary could learn if only she came to school regularly.

The major problem Mary's teacher, Barbara Wayne, faced was that Mary rarely came to school. By December she had been absent forty of seventy days of school. Helen was extremely concerned. She did not feel that she should recommend her for an educational evaluation until at least Mary's teacher had a fair opportunity to teach her and see if she could learn.

Helen tried to contact Mary's mother, but she did not have a phone and never answered the notes sent home. When the mother came in once a month to sign the welfare program's required school attendance form, Helen tried to convince her to get Mary to school more often so she could help her to learn. She knew that Mary's teacher was an outstanding teacher and could help Mary to improve tremendously if the child would only come to school.

Mary continued her pattern of excessive absence. Helen decided that perhaps if she threatened not to sign the school attendance form the mother

53

might get Mary to school more often. Helen informed her secretary that when the mother came to pick up the form in January, she wanted to speak to the mother so she could tell her she was not going to sign the form. Helen hoped that this threat would convince the mother to get Mary to school every day. Getting that signed form seemed to be the only thing that mattered to the mother. The principal intended to use it as an incentive to get Mary to school regularly.

When the mother came to the school in January, she came to the principal's office and Helen told the mother she had a wonderful daughter who was far behind academically and that the school wanted to help Mary to learn. The mother asked for the attendance form necessary for the welfare office. Helen refused to give it to her until she showed that she would get Mary to school each day.

The next day, Helen received a phone call from a social worker telling her that she must sign the form and give it to the mother. Helen knew the regulation that she must sign the form each month. All the mother had to do was to have the child registered in the school. Helen felt that registering a child is not enough and that the child must also attend school regularly. The social worker threatened to go to a judge to get her to sign the form. The social worker was correct according to the regulations at that time.

Well, Helen did sign the form and did so with a heavy heart. She told the classroom teacher, Barbara Wayne, what had occurred, and Barbara appreciated the fact that Helen did make a serious effort to do something to get Mary to come to school. Shortly afterward, Mary's mother took her out of school.

Most educators are sincere in their efforts to help children to learn. More and more society is requiring the parent or parents of a child to cooperate in order to maximize the achievement of the child's potential.

When teachers put forth a monumental effort and children come to school consistently and also put forth a superb effort, fabulous things occur. And, when the parents cooperate with the school, wonderful things can also happen. When the youngster does not get to school, it is impossible for the teacher to accomplish his or her goals.

When a parent does not cooperate, there should be some mechanism to motivate him or her to get the children to school. In the case of Mary, there was a nurturing school, a kind, highly proficient teacher, and an environment where she could have made splendid progress.

QUESTIONS

1. What could the legislature or court system do to support the school in a case like this?
2. What other strong actions could the principal have taken?
3. What programs or meetings could have been established to reach out to Mary's mother?

COMMENTS

Legislatures and courts must be more attuned to what teachers and school administrators need to do to educate children. There are too many examples of mandates, laws, and regulations that work against the wishes of school staff needs. Legislative and court officials need to articulate with schools and listen to school employees. Somehow there needs to be much more dialogue. Lastly, legislative and court officials need to have more respect for what school employees are trying to do and be more cooperative so that the schools can accomplish what society wants the schools to do.

Helen could have put Mary in a different class if she thought that would have had an impact on the mother. Perhaps Helen could have called in the social worker for a discussion to involve that agency in this case to get the child to school more often.

Perhaps the school psychologist could have talked to the mother. Also, the family worker or other community liaison could have visited the home and helped the mother to get the child to school.

Helen could have started group meetings with all families whose children have poor attendance and perhaps the group could have come up with ways to improve attendance. Helen might have assigned someone to this family to counsel the mother. Perhaps when the mother was in the school, the school secretary could have called Barbara Wayne to meet with the mother. Maybe meeting with the teacher would have helped the mother to see the importance of getting Mary to school. The teacher could have also explained what Mary is missing out on. If the school or district has an attendance teacher, that person might have intervened to help get Mary to school.

Chapter Thirteen

School Leadership Committee

Principal Mario Adamo felt that the Hunter School had been running well for several years with him at the helm. However, status quo was not what he wanted. He envisioned that new school improvements could be achieved if he formed a School Leadership Committee made up of various constituents. He had a fine student council that made many marvelous recommendations over the years, and now would be a good time to initiate a leadership committee.

Mario asked the parents to elect or select three parents for this committee. He asked the teachers to use the same process with their colleagues. He asked the aides, custodians, and lunchroom and office staff to select three representatives. The parents decided to select three parents from the parents' association executive board. The teachers elected three of their colleagues. One was from the lower grades. One was from the upper grades, and one represented the out-of-classroom teachers (those who taught the special subjects such as library, art, music, physical education, and science).

Mario called the district and reported his plan to Deputy Superintendent James Bell, who thought it was a great idea. He informed Mario that the district would be implementing such a plan the following September for all of the schools. James stated that the leadership committees were becoming a trend throughout the country because research demonstrated the value of collaboration in matters of school governance.

As Mario walked to the first meeting, he was enthusiastic and hopeful that this committee would suggest innovative improvements and work toward implementation of the recommendations. He had hoped that there would be a new influx of ideas and energy to make a good school even better. Mario knew that this school was not a perfect one, and he believed that with mature and constructive brainstorming, he could make the school more effective.

The first meeting was typical of those to follow. Two parents, Janice Callow and Tanya Page, suggested that parents should work on getting a traffic light for a busy street near the school. There had been several near misses of children getting hit by cars. These youngsters who walked to school needed a traffic light as well as the crossing guard who worked conscientiously there for years. The third parent, Martha Biggs, sat silent. The rest of the committee thought it was a great idea. The teachers suggested that the weakest area of the curriculum, science, receive a comprehensive evaluation and upgrading. The rest of the committee, except for Martha Biggs, thought it was a necessary area for serious consideration. At this point, Mrs. Biggs spoke up boldly: "Once again these teachers are saying they will fix the science program. I've heard that before." The science program had been a weak spot because the last two teachers who taught science left the school. One left because her husband landed a job in another state and the other because of illness.

The three teachers each took a turn explaining that everyone was aware that science was the weak area of the curriculum and that they were serious about "fixing" the science instruction in the school. They were prepared to get help from colleagues to search other science programs in surrounding schools. They were going to visit the publishers' booths at conferences to see what new materials were available, and they were going to seek out speakers to come to the teachers' meetings at the school to demonstrate exciting hands-on activities for teaching science. Mario was delighted to hear the enthusiasm the teachers shared, and he had a wonderful feeling that the science program would genuinely be improved. Janice Callow and Tanya Page smiled with delight because they sensed that there would be real improvement toward making science as good as the other curriculum areas.

"I think the teachers are on their way to solving the science problem," said Janice Callow.

"I certainly agree," stated Tanya Page.

"Well, I will hold off making a judgment until I see the results," said Martha Biggs.

The meeting ended with the representatives of the custodian, office staff, and lunchroom staff stating that they would each like to visit the classrooms or lead an assembly to help the youngsters understand their roles in the school.

QUESTIONS

1. Was it a good idea for Mario Adamo to convene such a committee? Why?

2. What is the best way to handle a parent like Martha Biggs who may be negative throughout all the committee meetings?
3. What could help this committee accomplish a great deal?
4. What could prevent the committee from getting anything accomplished?

COMMENTS

It was an excellent idea for Mario to launch such a brainstorming committee. He knew that after being in the school for several years he needed the input of others to continue to keep the school well run. He also knew that by involving others it would increase their pride and help them to see that their ideas and opinions were worthwhile and welcomed. Lastly, it is obvious that there is a problem with the science program. Perhaps with the help of the committee Mario could improve the overall science instruction as well as accomplish many other goals for the school. Mario is well aware that no one person can solve all the problems. Many individuals working together can increase harmony while achieving solutions necessary for the best interests of the students.

The principal must keep calm when Martha Biggs complains. He also has to work hard to make sure that the committee sets up goals and works to achieve them and finds ways to show parents like Martha Biggs that the school can improve. He needs to follow through on the committee decisions as well as to see to it that committee members do what they say they need to do. Once there is a sufficient number of goals achieved, parents like Martha Biggs will be satisfied and may even become more optimistic about what the principal and other staff members can accomplish for the children.

If the members of the committee are serious and truly want to do something for the benefit of the school, much can be achieved. The committee has to set goals that are relevant and realistic. The committee has to set up timetables for each set of goals. It needs to meet regularly and give the members a chance to explain what they are doing and what the roadblocks are. The committee has to report regularly to their constituencies so everyone knows what is going on and what the eventual outcome will be. In addition, the committee members need to hear from their constituencies. They should bring concerns by the general population to the meetings so that those not on the committee feel they have input. Also the committee must be careful not to take on too much at one time so that goals are achievable. Lastly, totally irrelevant items need to be avoided.

Nothing will be accomplished if each person does not do what he or she volunteers to do. Someone has to verify that each person is acting on the decision she or he promised to work on. In addition, little will be achieved if there is bickering and a lack of consensus. Pessimism and giving reasons why things cannot get done will hinder the process and lead to little progress. Lastly, the committee cannot allow any setbacks to decrease motivation to discuss, make decisions, assign jobs and complete them, and evaluate what the new achievements have done for the benefit of the school.

Chapter Fourteen

A Principal's Report Card

As a community leader, as a religious person, and especially as a professional educator working with children, Sal Turso knew the importance of ethical considerations in decision making. His father, a medical doctor, often spoke of the Hippocratic oath: first, do no harm. His training and experiences reinforced in Sal that ancient dictum. As an educator, Sal tried to keep in mind the best interests of children as he made decisions. As much as he tried to adopt an ethical base in his decision-making framework, Sal also felt keen pressure to improve student achievement levels. His superintendent, Rose Delvecchio, demanded increased performance. "Their performance, Sal, is your report card," she would often tell him.

Sal's commitment to ethics was soon put to the test. This dilemma came to a head when Sal received a grant of $50,000 to develop an after-school tutoring program for thirty students who needed extra help. Regina Hitchcock, the guidance counselor, urged him to include in the program children who suffered poor interpersonal skills, had few friends, and whose home lives often disrupted their learning. "They need extra help to compensate for the turmoil at home," she said to Sal. She added, "Besides, if we keep them after school, we can feed them and give them more structure than they would receive after school playing and getting into mischief on the mean streets." Sal knew she had a point. He knew well how dangerous the streets were and that schools needed to be responsible for the social and emotional well-being of their students. The idea that today's school did not end at three o'clock was part of Sal's core beliefs.

Sal's dilemma increased slightly when Mary Cassidy sent him a memo on the subject of who should be included in the tutoring. Mary urged the principal to restrict selection to those students who would benefit the most from the tutoring. She reasoned that since the school would be judged based on the achievement of students, it made sense to include only youngsters who, with concentrated and highly focused instruction on test-taking skills, could reach passing level. Sal always respected Mary as a clear thinker who knew how to get the best results for the school. Quick math on his part helped him understand her logic. Only forty students in the group of one hundred students were reading on grade level. It made sense to identify for the thirty slots those students who had the best shot of passing the test. If even twenty students in the tutoring classes of thirty could pass the test with the strategies that Mary recommended, that would still be a jump of 20 percent to a far more competitive 60 percent student success rate. The superintendent would be pleased and the pressure on Sal and the teachers would abate.

Next, Florence Kaye weighed in with her views on how the money should be spent. Florence, a widely respected teacher, argued that her students were learning disabled and suffering severe behavioral disorders. She urged tutoring for her students as a matter of equity. Sal, a former special education teacher, sympathized with her fervent pleas. He also was concerned that her students were so hopelessly behind in their studies that the tutoring program would not sufficiently prepare them for the new tests—tests that would reflect on his ability as principal to increase pupil achievement on the upcoming standardized test scores. Student success, or failure, would well determine Sal's success, or failure, as a principal.

QUESTIONS

1. To what extent should student social-emotional well-being play in Sal's decision in this case?
2. How much consideration should Sal give to Florence Kaye's argument for equity?
3. Evaluate Mary Cassidy's arguments on the basis of ethics, equity, and the need to increase the numbers of children passing the test.
4. If you were principal, how would you respond to Sal's dilemma? What action would you take?
5. How practical is ethics as a general principle of decision making?
6. What alternatives might be available in Sal's struggle to resolve his dilemma?

COMMENTS

This case illustrates one of many Hobbesian choices that administrators must make under the No Child Left Behind Act. As a school leader Sal is confronting the dilemma of choosing between his personal priorities and values and the equally compelling need to foster greater pupil performance. The ambivalence he faces is compounded by the sanctions for poor achievement that can be imposed on a school as a result of the increasing accountability demands of No Child Left Behind.

Schools like Sal's that receive federal reimbursement and extra services to educate large numbers of at-risk students have a great deal at stake in this ongoing battle to raise achievement levels. If, for example, a school falls short of meeting its yearly progress goals for several consecutive years, a wide range of penalties can be decided. These penalties may range from technical assistance from the central office to replacement of the principal and up to 50 percent of the faculty, or to the more stringent consolidation or closing down of the school.

With such draconian penalties, Sal must base his decision on the greater good. Which approach—Regina's emphasis on the social-emotional needs of students, Mary's emphasis on pragmatism, or Florence's call for equity— should Sal adopt? In resolving this dilemma Sal must ask himself several questions that will guide his decision making: What criteria have been devised for participation in the tutoring program? Is a class size of thirty its own recipe for program failure? Are other funds available to create another class? What support services in the form of extra staffing will the tutoring program provide to help students with social-emotional needs or those who are learning disabled or have behavior problems? If money for support service is budgeted for the program, how much? Can Sal trade the support money for other services? Can the school provide other remediation assistance for those who ultimately are not selected for the after-school tutoring program? After pondering all these issues, Sal may well conclude the pressure to produce wields the heaviest weight in his final decision. Confronted with the No Child Left Behind Act that requires consistent increases in the number of children passing the standardized tests, Sal will likely adopt Mary's logic and aim to get "the most bang for the buck." His reasoning here is that students who nearly passed the tests last year have a greater potential to pass this year's exams—although they may not be the students in the greatest need of help. Sal will explain to his faculty that in order to avoid the sanctions of No Child Left Behind, the school must follow a strategy that will yield the highest impact on scores.

Many administrators in Sal's position would likely agree with this strategy. The new focus on pushing students on the cusp over the threshold to success may be an unintended consequence of a law that places the highest priority on test scores, admittedly a narrow criterion of school effectiveness. Because administrators may be adopting this shortcut to success, there may be little incentive to work with students at the bottom to improve their performance—or, for that matter, students who are excelling in standardized tests.

Sal, and other school leaders, must know that his strategy in this case will yield only some short-term success because under the terms of the No Child Left Behind legislation, *all* students must at least score at a "proficient" level by the 2013–2014 school year. Schools can no longer identify or target specific groups to maximize school results at the expense of other groups of students. Schools must begin to attend to all students, irrespective of race, language, gender, or handicapping condition, and to ensure that all groups pass standardized tests.

The law's expectation that all children will become proficient within the next several years has become known as Annual Yearly Progress (AYP). This is the new yardstick that will determine the quality of a school. Although the 2013–2014 timeline is fixed, individual states set their own standards of proficiency. States may also choose their own tests, thereby permitting additional flexibility. Perhaps the most complex aspect of the law is the specification of how much progress is considered adequate. This leaves room for various interpretations on a state-by-state basis.

A report released by the Education Commission of the States (ECS) details the steps that all fifty states have taken to comply with the No Child Left Behind legislation and outlines how far each state still has to go before reaching full compliance with the law. School administrators will want to review the requirements of the law and how each state is progressing to meet the law's demands.

REFERENCE

Education Commission of the States. Available at www.ecs.org.

Chapter Fifteen

Will Cheating Strike Out Bobby?

Early one Monday morning Tim Davidson was just sitting down to enjoy the nice cup of hazelnut coffee he had prepared for himself when Rick Larsen, dean of students, interrupted his moment of peace. "You better sit down," Rick advised his principal. "We have a problem."

Rick went on to explain his dilemma. According to Rick, teacher Jane Barton was reviewing the results of a social studies project that required students to conduct oral interviews with senior citizens in the community and with several civic leaders. The interviews were all part of an assignment to research the history of the town. While examining the student reports, Jane noticed that Bobby Henson's project appeared very similar to another report that she had read. Upon investigation, Jane concluded that Bobby's work was an exact replica of the same assignment she administered two years ago when she taught Bobby's older brother Mark. When she confronted Bobby, he broke down and admitted he plagiarized the assignment. He did so because he had no time to do the assignment since the school's baseball team kept him busy. Bobby, by all accounts, was a star player on the team.

Dean Larsen added that Jane was planning to give Bobby a failing grade for cheating on the assignment. Since the project counted for more than half of his final grade, Bobby's failure meant that he would be required to attend summer school. Her decision to fail Bobby was consistent with the student handbook that stated "as part of the school's policy to maintain standards of personal honesty, cheating of any kind may require a failing grade by the teacher."

"So what's the problem?" Tim asked his friend Rick. "Bobby cheated and he broke an important school rule. He should fail." "Hold it," Rick interjected. "Tim, you should know that Bobby's uncle is Mr. Michaels, the president of the local Chamber of Commerce that sponsors our school's baseball team. He also is an outspoken member of the Board of Education. If Bobby has to attend summer school, he cannot participate in the summer baseball tournament, which means a lot to the kids and their families. And that tournament sure helps our kids get scholarships to some mighty fine schools."

Tim pushed aside the coffee he no longer had an appetite for. In a meeting the very next day with Jane, she informed Tim that she expected the school administration to uphold the school's handbook's ban on cheating.

Molly Scott, the union representative for the teachers, accompanied Jane to her meeting with the principal. They reminded Tim that Bobby and his mom had signed a letter indicating awareness of the contents of the hand-book.

Unsure how to proceed with the dilemma that ruined his appetite for coffee and later would ruin his week, Tim called the superintendent, Irv Miller, for advice. Irv counseled Tim, "As the chief exec of your school, you make your decision as you deem fit, but my advice is to be careful, Tim. You know how passionate Mr. Michaels gets about all the benefits sports bring to our town and our kids."

QUESTIONS

1. What options does Tim have as he tries to resolve this case?
2. Evaluate these options and suggest a best plan of recourse for Tim.

COMMENTS

This case is fraught with logistical, political, and ethical implications for Tim. As he navigates his path toward a solution, he was wise enough to inform his superintendent about this dilemma. A smart administrator is always advised to communicate complex issues with one's superior. Tim passed that test when he called Irv.

Cheating often begins in elementary school when students seek a competitive edge in games and in their studies. It peaks in middle and high schools when approximately three of four students admit to some form of academic dishonesty.

Perhaps the most vexing conclusion of research on cheating is not so much the increasing frequency with which it takes place, but the indifferent reactions on the part of educators about cheating. Cheating appears to be a common response to external pressures or to one's own inadequacies. Bobby, for example, admitted to cheating because the pressure of baseball occupied a lot of his time. At the outset Tim will want to investigate the amount of time that the baseball team consumes for all the players.

Now Tim must address the substantive issue of Bobby's cheating. At first glance this appears to be an open-and-shut case. Bobby cheated, admitted he cheated, and the policy was clear with respect to the consequences. But was the policy really clear?

Upon further reflection, one would conclude the policy does have some flexibility through the "wiggle room" clause that states that "cheating of any kind may require a failing grade by the teacher." Given this significant clause, the principal does have several options to pursue as he explores a resolution. Tim can, of course, support the teacher and enforce the policy against cheating. He might also ask Jane if she could recommend other possible solutions. Repeating the course with another teacher, permitting Bobby to do an independent study project, suspending Bobby, and suggesting he lose credit for the assignment are alternatives that Jane and Tim may wish to consider. Given the intensity of her feelings in this case, it is unlikely that these are viable options for Tim as principal.

Tim faces a conflict between his administrative duty to enforce policy and perhaps personal anxiety that are compounded by ethical and political ramifications. Such conflict is often the crux of decision making. According to Hodgkinson, "values, morals and ethics are the very stuff of leadership and administrative life" (1991, 11). Ethics begins where policies and rules leave off.

It would be quite easy for Tim to apply the wiggle room clause and broker a solution acceptable to all parties. In following this approach, however, Tim may lose the trust relationship he has with his faculty. While the larger society continues to witness a steady deterioration of trust in its leaders, trust is the anchor of a caring and concerned school. In recent years we have seen a reporter plagiarize his stories for a world famous newspaper. We have seen a well-respected presidential historian lift whole sections of research for a book she was writing without giving credit to the researchers. We have seen professors and athletic coaches lie about their professional credentials. We have seen top executives of major corporations falsify company reports. The trend away from trust on the grounds that "everyone does it" or "nobody would get hurt" cannot be used to rationalize such conduct.

Trust presents a special challenge for school administrators because the lack of trust is all too prevalent in so many societal institutions. Educational leaders can only be effective if the school community sees them as operating within an environment of trust, respect, and honesty.

One authority on trust in schools, Megan Tschannen-Moran, noted, "school leaders who . . . earn the trust of members of their school community are in a better position to accomplish the complex task of educating a diverse group of students in a changing world. . . . These leaders also create the conditions that foster trust between teachers, including structures and norms for behavior, and they assist them in resolving the inevitable conflicts that arise" (2004, 12).

The structure and norms are clearly in place at Tim's school, and he is honor bound to adhere to the school policy despite the wiggle room clause. To do otherwise and attempt to work out an arrangement with Mr. Michaels could result in an inflammation of the issue and cause long-term embarrassment to the entire school district and to the parties in this case. The mere whiff of an accommodation on Bobby's behalf by ignoring the policy or tweaking it to help Bobby and appease his uncle will only reinforce public perception about too many of our leaders being immoral or corrupt in their thinking and their actions. Neither Tim nor the district needs that perception.

As a final element in his decision-making process, Tim would be wise again to share his conclusions with the superintendent about the need to enforce the school policy. This is as much a matter of trust between superintendent and principal as it is a matter of strategy for Irv. Upon learning of Tim's decision, Irv must contact Mr. Michaels to explain to him the issues and ramifications. Irv, himself a trustworthy leader, must hold fast to his professional values and support Tim. To do otherwise and seek political accommodation with Mr. Michaels may compromise Irv's capacity for effective leadership.

REFERENCES

Hodgkinson, C. 1991. *Educational leadership: The moral art.* Albany, NY: State University of New York Press.

Tschannen-Moran, M. 2004. *Trust matters: leadership for successful schools.* San Francisco, CA: Jossey-Bass.

Chapter Sixteen

The Chart Attack

"Make no mistake, ladies and gentlemen. Parents, the superintendent, the entire community are all demanding an improvement. We cannot sit by and allow student achievement to suffer. Everyone wants results, and we need to show results. We will be under attack if we don't improve."

Using a PowerPoint presentation to outline a five-year review of results on standardized tests, school principal Joan Jimenez laid out for the faculty at its monthly conference the seriousness of the problem. For too long, scores had suffered at Blackstone School, and the Board of Education was pressuring for improvement. If achievement levels did not rise, the central office was considering transferring faculty and administrators.

Cathy Amante's hand quickly shot up. The faculty representative responded passionately to the principal's comments. "This used to be a fun place to work. We all enjoyed coming to work. Faculty meetings were a place to discuss mutual concerns between teachers and administration. We even had a few minutes to celebrate birthdays, weddings, family events. Now all we discuss is scores and standards. Every meeting we pore over new statistics, recent trends, achievement percentages, improvement percentages, progress indicators, weekly, monthly, quarterly, semester, and annual performance reviews. Our morale is shot. We're under attack alright. A chart attack!"

When Cathy finished voicing her concerns about the direction that Blackstone was moving, the principal surveyed faculty reaction across the room. She quickly saw the nodding of heads and quiet murmurs of agreement. The anxiety from faculty was palpable. As Blackstone's principal for the past six years, Joan worked hard to instill a positive culture in the school. She respected the faculty for its diligence in helping students and the family bonds they felt for their colleagues. Celebrations were but one of several tools she used to advance the notion of collegiality and team work.

New accountability requirements imposed by No Child Left Behind legislation were forcing Joan to reconsider her leadership style. Perhaps her collaborative leadership was not the best method to secure compliance with the new government edicts. Maybe she should simply send a memo to faculty and staff directing them to comply with the new initiatives that emphasized data, results, and scores. She felt conflicted in her desire to maintain a vibrant school culture while confronting all the demands for heightened school accountability. As sympathetic as she was to faculty sentiment, Joan also knew the serious consequences if her school continued its downward slide.

In her attempt to come to terms with the age of accountability, Joan had to confront her long cherished educational values. She believed, for example, in educating the whole child and always thought that art, music, student debate teams, and sports programs might reclaim their rightful place in the curriculum. She was as concerned for the social-emotional development of her students as she was for their academic achievement. But she fretted that the pressure for scores was beginning to crowd out other curriculum areas.

Joan's anxiety only deepened when she encountered Nancy Turley in the local supermarket. Nancy, the always pleasant eighth-grader with her cherubic face and ever-ready smile, told her principal she was planning to quit the school's soccer team and the cheerleading squad. "Too much homework. And my mom says I have to study for all the big tests this year," said Nancy.

QUESTIONS

1. What role does data play in school decision making?
2. How can schools use data to promote greater academic achievement levels?
3. Should Joan change her leadership style and simply direct teachers to implement new decisions-by-data priorities?

COMMENTS

The inexorable push toward increased school accountability is greater than ever before. This is but one of several major policy adjustments in the wake of the No Child Left Behind legislation. Whatever anxiety Blackstone's teachers and principal are having in relation to performance and overall assessment of student progress is the same heated debate taking place at virtually every school in the nation. No Child Left Behind has changed the rules of school and student success.

Scores, ratings, and achievement data are now the norm that boards of education, the public, and the media use to evaluate schools.

In many ways schools are like the poignant scene in Lewis Carroll's Alice's *Adventures in Wonderland* when Alice asked the Cheshire Cat for directions. "Would you please tell me which way I ought to go from here?" asked Alice. "That depends a good deal on where you want to get to," replied the cat. Many of us do not quite know in which direction we want schools to go. We also do not know where we are now. There are as many who will argue that academic achievement should be the primary responsibility of schools as there are others who will argue that producing good citizens should be the objective of schools. Still others note the need for schools to inculcate in students proper social-emotional development. No Child Left Behind may have settled this long-standing debate, at least temporarily.

The faculty conference is a powerful forum to determine school goals and how to use data to get there. During this meeting time teachers have the opportunity to discuss the curriculum, recommend appropriate instructional strategies, and design tools for proper assessment. Teachers can also analyze work samples and identify intervention measures where necessary. Charts provide useful information on the number and percentage of students who attain desired performance levels.

Faculty, department, and grade level meetings enable teachers to continually review their pacing schedules to be sure students reach target goals for each grading period. The data help not only to place students in the appropriate groups but also to help teachers determine areas of student weakness and to inform teachers of areas in which to adjust instruction.

The entire teaching-learning process that characterizes data-driven schools possesses several important features:

• Review of curriculum standards in each subject area;
• Determination of specific student outcomes for each subject;
• Development of common examinations, making assessment easier;
• Analysis of exam results;
• Identification of student weaknesses;
• Implementation of intervention strategies to help students.

This process offers several benefits for teachers and students alike that include more focused methods of instruction, improved learning for students, identification of curriculum areas in need of review, better testing measures, and a clearer measure of school effectiveness.

As principal, Joan must find ways to create a team effort if the faculty is to make good use of the vast amounts of school data available. Her emphasis on data must become their priority. She must persuade, not order, faculty. Joan must work with faculty to coordinate the school's vision statement with data. If Blackstone School wants better achievement levels, it must start with the data. The use of school data information allows faculty and the principal to set goals and examine progress toward the goals.

Team members can ask themselves several penetrating questions: Why are we teaching this material? How does it align with expected outcomes? Why do we use the strategies we do? What works and doesn't work in teaching this material? What percentage of students is performing satisfactorily on key evaluation measures? Did students perform better this year than last? Why? Why not? What corrections are needed? Reflective questions such as these will encourage introspective analysis by faculty.

Joan must work with teachers in this newfound mission to use data to spur student achievement. She needs to reflect on several issues too: What support services, such as common schedules, release time, additional staffing, or professional development, do the teachers need? What aspects of the curriculum should be emphasized? What ideas should the school celebrate through ceremonies and rituals? How can she demonstrate consistency in communicating her priorities? How will she address poor performance?

Joan must begin to recognize and reward faculty for its commitment to the new emphasis on data collection and use. In his best-selling book *1001 Ways to Reward Employees*, Bob Nelson observed that "recognition for a job well done is the top motivator of employee performance" (1994, xv). Ironically, Lortie and Evans found that although such recognition was essential to higher performance, it was virtually unheard of in school settings (as in Schmoker 1999, 111–115; 2001). Joan must avoid this trap of taking teachers for granted.

Joan must also avoid any tendency to use data as a hammer to punish teachers whose results may not measure up to her expectations. By embarrassing teachers, Joan may inadvertently promote a divisive, noncollaborative work environment. She must talk about continuous improvement and support. She must keep the focus on how best to help children in need. A focus on data will provide the direction.

REFERENCES

Nelson, B. 1994. *1001 ways to reward employees*. New York: Workman Press.
Schmoker, M. 1999. *Results: The key to continuous school improvement*, 2nd ed. Alexandria, VA: Association for Supervision and Curriculum Development.
Schmoker, M. 2001. *The results fieldbook: Practical strategies from dramatically improved schools*. Alexandria, VA: Association for Supervision and Curriculum Development.

Chapter Seventeen

Fighting Fat

"We're on overload already. How much more can the teachers do? Every time society sneezes, it lands on the school's nose. This is the straw that's gonna break the camel's back. Something's gotta give. . . . We can't do it all." Evelyn Lucamo, teacher representative at Allenville School, was rarely so agitated. The straw in this case is the recommendation by some parents that the school begin to address the obesity epidemic that has hit as many as ten million of the nation's school children including students at Allenville.

Seth Southworth, the longtime principal of Allenville, was sympathetic to Evelyn's thinking. He knew exactly what she meant about society's sneezing and its implications for the schools. When the country became aware of the AIDS epidemic, it was the schools that were required to set up AIDS awareness programs. When sexual harassment became an issue, the schools began sexual harassment training for faculty. When bullying came to the attention of the media, schools enacted an antibullying curriculum. And when the dangers of smoking became apparent to all, society turned to the schools to combat the problem.

Seth already had his hands full with the introduction of state standards into the schools, No Child Left Behind mandates, high-stakes testing, curriculum reform, assessments, shared decision-making initiatives plus the usual dilemmas of placing qualified teachers in every classroom, budget shortfalls, an ever-increasing volume of paperwork, and motivating his senior staff. He knew also Evelyn's comments about an overworked faculty were very much on target. In recent years they were constantly being asked to do more with less.

Yet Seth also knew the research and sobering statistics about the relationship between student health and academic success. Chronically malnourished children are more prone to become sick, miss classes, be absent from school, and ultimately perform more poorly than children who eat nutritious meals. He had just read a report from the federal Centers for Disease Control and Prevention noting that the rate of overweight children and adolescents between ages six and nineteen had nearly tripled in the past thirty years. He knew also of the testimony by the U.S. Surgeon General before a congressional subcommittee that obesity is "the fastest growing cause of disease and death in America." Seth was also aware that childhood obesity could lead to type 2 diabetes and heart disease. As a lifelong resident of Allenville, Seth was concerned about his neighbors. His students were their children.

But Seth did not need research or reports to tell him about Allenville's adiposity. Every day as he passed by the school cafeteria, he saw youngsters munching on bagels, pizza, chicken nuggets, candy, chips, fries, and soda—all high in fat and sugar. Vending machines filled with cookies, candy, and carbonated beverages were scattered about the school building. And the upcoming school fundraiser involved the sale of candy. Parent-teacher association meetings often included cake sales.

Seth tried to rationalize his concern for student health with the reality of running a school. After all, the annual candy sale and raffles brought in much needed revenue to purchase badly needed school equipment. He could not count on the school's budget allocation from the central office to pay for office supplies like paper, toner for the copy machine, and especially the insurance agreement he had with the copy machine salesman for twenty-four-hour repair service. Petty cash derived from vending machines helped to pay for the certificates, trophies, and plaques that were all a part of Allenville's student awards program. And Seth was always being asked to find money for the handful of students who could not afford school trips. He needed that money to run his school!

When he was not wrestling with his need for petty cash to operate a school with over two thousand high school teenagers, Seth, ever mindful of the pressure to raise achievement scores, found himself pondering the more basic question that Evelyn was asking: "How much more can the teachers do?"

QUESTIONS

1. To what extent are social issues like obesity, smoking, and bullying the responsibility of the school?
2. Knowing faculty resentment about any new curriculum, should Seth proceed with an antiobesity curriculum? Why? Why not?
3. How should Seth address the issue of general faculty overload?

4. What is the role of parents and the larger community in addressing social issues?
5. How can the principal educate his faculty to know the importance of nutrition as a factor in pupil achievement?

COMMENTS

In addressing this problem, Seth must contend with several issues: (1) the philosophical question of whether it is the school's responsibility to tackle yet another societal ill; (2) the resistance of faculty to another task; (3) the best strategy to mount a nutrition education program; and (4) revenue options to fund necessary school programs.

As much as Seth may feel the pressure to focus on student achievement, he must also know that schools exist for more than academic success. Schools of today have more responsibilities thrust on them than ever before. The inculcation of civic awareness, development of student self-esteem, socialization skills, and proper work habits are all a part of the school's broader mission. Society views educational institutions as transmitters of its social values. When societal needs change, schools must adapt to that change.

Seth must also know that any school improvement plan that does not take into account the myriad other factors that impact learning is a myopic view. Proper nutrition and diet are among those factors that affect student achievement. Students spend up to one-third of their entire day in school. They are greatly influenced by what they do and what they experience in school.

Seth faces some practical obstacles to any ideas he might offer to tackle student adiposity. These obstacles include faculty resistance and the related concern about an overcrowded curriculum. To add another component to the curriculum may well be, as the teacher representative Evelyn Lucamo warns, "the straw that's gonna break the camel's back." He must be sensitive to faculty concerns about yet another curriculum add-on that may threaten the primary goal of academic achievement. He must also be sensitive to the needs of the at-risk students as they relate to overall success in school.

Seth would do well to convene an advisory committee of teachers, the school nurse, and other support staff, parents, and students to explore the scope of the problem and to promote alternative eating behaviors among students. At the outset the committee should tap into the resources of local hospitals and universities to obtain assistance from nutritionists on staff. A nutritionist might be available both as a committee member and as a resource for faculty, parents, and children too.

This committee should consider ways in which the school itself contributes to the problem. The committee may find, for example, that the school environment exacerbates the problem of poor nutrition by the limited menu in the lunchroom, or the vending machines that entice students in every corner of the building. The committee should also examine student, staff, and parent attitudes about nutrition. In an attitudinal survey of staff, parents, and students, the committee may find that adult willingness, perhaps eagerness, to eat junk food may send the wrong message to students.

After a review of the surveys, the committee should develop its recommendations. Aware of the danger of faculty overload, the committee might consider a curricular and extracurricular response. The curricular response would consist of units of study emphasizing nutrition, diet, exercise, and healthy lifestyles in the physical education programs. Other curriculum areas lend themselves to an interdisciplinary approach. In the science class, for example, students could examine medical data that have determined positive correlations between student fitness and academic achievement. In math class, students might track weight and body mass index. Guidance classes might plan activities to increase student self-esteem and understanding of others.

Another response would entail an extracurricular program in the form of an afterschool club for students identified as at-risk of obesity. Funding for this initiative might come from local and government grants. Parents would be welcome as participants or as volunteers to run the program. Some activities might include basketball, jumping rope, one-on-one sessions, and training on how to select and prepare healthy meals, and how to distinguish between media advertising of food and truth-in-advertising claims. Student councils might sponsor Walk for Life Campaigns to reward students who maintain a daily half-hour exercise routine with their picture on a sneaker bulletin board.

As principal, Seth can use his leadership ability to create an attractive cafeteria with menu choices and give students more time to eat. The typical school cafeteria is overcrowded and may take students as long as twenty minutes to be served. The result is a stressful and unpleasant eating experience. Seth might also work with the advisory committee to stock the vending machines with healthy snacks and beverages. Examples of these nutritious foods include low-fat cookies, dried fruits, trail mix, baked chips, popcorn, water, and 100 percent fruit juices. Fundraisers should focus on nonfood items as other revenue sources. Magazine sales, boosters, raffles, silent auctions, and general donations are possibilities.

Chapter Eighteen

Town on the Rebound?

For over twenty years the town of Hartsville had enjoyed a record of academic success for its students. This working-class community provided steady employment and generous fringe benefits for employees thanks largely to the significant presence of an auto manufacturing plant. Many graduates of Hartsville schools had elected to remain in the community to become part of its workforce and to settle down in the town they loved. They hoped the schools would educate their own children as it had educated them a generation ago.

The prosperity and the stability that the community had come to expect did not continue due to changing economics and competition from foreign cars. Just as the townspeople had to tighten their belts, so too did the Hartsville Board of Education, which prided itself on a series of annual budgets that barely kept pace with inflation. The once-thriving Hartsville schools had begun to cut back on exemplary academic initiatives and extracurricular activities. Popular athletic programs, driver education, all-day kindergarten, and advanced placement courses for high school students were but a few of the casualties. Class size was on the increase, and teacher salaries fell below the median range for the state. Student discipline became a source of growing concern, and vandalism in and about school property became more apparent. Absenteeism on the part of faculty and students became more noticeable. Worse still, the cost-conscious Board of Education imposed spending freezes almost as an annual rite of every spring. They did so because expenses outstripped revenues with every passing year. In the past year alone, computer upgrades, building repairs, and adult education programs were all put on hold pending some last minute infusion of cash from the state legislature.

Despite these challenges, numerous civic, business, and fraternal organizations maintained a presence in the town. They provided resources and services whenever possible. They pledged ongoing support in an open letter to the Board of Education. At the same time, their patience increasingly tested by the onslaught of problems facing the schools, the town leaders urged corrective action.

The ever-proud school board, wanting the best for its residents and students, knew it had to act decisively to restore the schools to their former status and elevate the entire Hartsville school system to the higher standards demanded for success in the twenty-first century. Board President Yvette Clovers directed Superintendent Jacqueline Henry to devise a complete educational renewal plan within ninety days to address the numerous issues confronting the Board of Education and Hartsville.

The superintendent took to the assignment with great enthusiasm. In fact, she was hired less than one year ago from another state precisely because she displayed a visionary approach to education and was enthusiastic in all that she did. She possessed a prodigious work ethic and a true desire to see Hartsville on the rebound.

Jacqueline met with her immediate staff at central office and hammered out an extensive list of recommendations. A portion of the menu for improvement included:

1. Introduction of a district-wide Code of Conduct.
2. Realignment of all central office staff to ensure greater support for the schools.
3. Reform of the entire K-12 curriculum to include more rigor and more writing.
4. Partnership with the local university professors to implement all curriculum changes.
5. A public relations campaign to educate the community to the tradition of success that Hartsville has known for many years.
6. Appointment of a full-time grants writer to secure foundation and government grants for school programs.
7. A regular series of community outreach programs including town meetings, monthly community newsletter, and community forums to address plans for improvement.
8. Substantial investment in technology to be funded through a school bond issue.
9. A five-year capital improvement plan for building repairs and construction.

The superintendent's list included explicit plans, a well-defined timetable for implementation, and revenue sources to carry out the recommendations. In keeping with the overall goal to revamp the educational programs, she also revised the vision statement for the entire school district. This was the first such revision in over ten years.

True to the ninety-day mandate, the superintendent submitted her Hartsville Optimism for People Empowerment (HOPE) plan to Board President Clovers and her six colleagues on the board. The plan was greeted with general board approval.

QUESTIONS

1. Describe the superintendent's leadership style. Is it appropriate for this situation?
2. Analyze the process that the superintendent used to develop the HOPE plan.
3. Can you suggest alternative approaches that the superintendent might have found helpful?
4. What degree of success can the superintendent expect when the Board of Education gives its okay for implementation?
5. If you were a member of the central planning team, what advice would you offer the superintendent?

COMMENTS

Based on the superintendent's activities thus far, the Hartsville Board of Education can be assured that Jacqueline will display a peripatetic pace in her efforts to reform the schools. Indeed, she exudes confidence, ideas, vision, and energy. These are all qualities of leadership. While she has outlined an ambitious agenda described in the HOPE plan, a more fundamental question is whether her strategy is smart.

Jacqueline represents the "great person" leadership style of the past. Under the great person theory, educational problems could be resolved by a powerful individual who would bring strong personal and professional qualities to the task at hand. This style—typical of leaders in the 1970s and 1980s—has given way to more recent research that validates the strategy of shared decision making. Community support is crucial for any lasting decisions, but any plan to revamp the schools without community involvement is a formula for failure. Jacqueline's plans for change, regardless of her personal strengths, may be doomed if she fails to secure community input. Current trends in leadership emphasize collaboration in decision making. If her plan is to succeed, Jacqueline must clearly engage the community.

The superintendent is presented in this case with the challenge of bringing together the entire community to meet the changing educational needs of Hartsville. The town's business and civic leadership has signaled its support for change. Jacqueline would be wise to harness that support. Any failure on her part to embrace and build on that support may well generate apathy at best and outright defiance at worst. Her role should be to serve as facilitator for improvement. In addition to convening her central office staff to brainstorm ideas, Jacqueline must make it a priority to tap into the talents and abilities of all stakeholders. The stakeholders would include school personnel, parents, community leaders, businesspeople, and perhaps students themselves. She might wish to engage the services of consultants in organizational change who would help her to define clear goals and work to encourage greater stakeholder involvement in the entire process. The successful adoption and implementation of the superintendent's HOPE plan depends as much on the participatory process she establishes as it does on the substance of her ideas and the ideas of others. She does not have a monopoly on wisdom, and the input of stakeholders may provide additional insights and solutions. Jacqueline needs to set up a team approach to enhance the likelihood of success. Otherwise, the plan becomes her plan, and she will have failed to capitalize on the resources of the larger community.

Chapter Nineteen

Making a Mark

Jeremy Rivera was a respected teacher at the Sawyer School. He had worked hard as a special education teacher and received professional recognition with his selection as Educator of the Year. Zachary Tuttle, his principal, noticed talent in the young Jeremy and tapped him as a person of strong potential to become a school administrator. The ever-willing Jeremy appreciated the confidence his principal had bestowed on him and quickly registered for graduate-level courses to study educational leadership at the local university.

Jeremy plunged into his assignments with his usual earnestness. He reveled in his coursework where he learned how to create a vision for his school. He learned new approaches to such vexing issues as low expectations for student achievement, motivation of a senior but unproductive staff, and innovative ways to spur parent involvement. His professors saw in Jeremy a committed educator who believed passionately in the power of education to improve the lives of children and the profession itself.

Shortly after attaining certification to become a school administrator, Jeremy again took his principal's advice and applied for a position as assistant principal at several schools that advertised vacancies. Jeremy hoped his new assignment would be similar to the enriching professional atmosphere he enjoyed at Sawyer with its long tradition of collaborative decision making and good faculty-student-administration-community relationships. In fact, the extraordinary relationship that existed between teachers and the principal allowed Jeremy to pursue innovative teaching ideas on behalf of his learning disabled and emotionally handicapped students. He was particularly proud of the support his principal had given him when he proposed the idea of setting up a student business as the curriculum focus for his classes. Knowing the special characteristics of his students and their need for a more reality-based curriculum that would make education come alive, Jeremy used the Sawyer School Student Store (a name created by students themselves to illustrate the literary technique of alliteration) to instruct his classes in mathematics, language arts, career education, and research. They learned new vocabulary like pricing, inventory, costs, profit, margin, advertising, volume, discount, and the power of advertising on the public address system. Every morning students could be heard hawking the day's products with special mention of the daily sale items.

The encouragement that Jeremy received from Zachary Tuttle made the young man realize the critical role school administrators play in improving educational opportunity for all students, especially those with special learning needs like his students. He vowed to apply his principal's philosophy of collaboration and support to his first supervisory position.

The Chapel School was Jeremy's first supervisory assignment, and he was eager to make his mark. His first meeting with his principal, Cecilia Toner, did not go well. She admitted upfront that she was troubled by his limited experience and relative youth. She added that the Board of Education had appointed Jeremy over her own recommendation, Ian Shaffer, who had given years of loyal and competent service to the Chapel School. "Ian was training for years for this position," explained Cecilia to her now despondent assistant principal. "Everybody here loves Ian. The parents, students, the faculty. We'll just have to make this thing work," shrugged Jeremy's boss.

QUESTIONS

1. Should Jeremy resign his position as assistant principal given the opposition to his appointment?
2. Why do you think the Board of Education appointed Jeremy as assistant principal over the objections of the principal?
3. Assume Jeremy decides to stay as assistant principal. What must he do "to make this thing work"? Be specific.
4. What should Cecilia do "to make this thing work"?

COMMENTS

Jeremy is in an unenviable position as the new assistant to a principal who is lukewarm to his appointment. Despite the less than sanguine position in which he finds himself, it would be premature for Jeremy to resign his position. The Board of Education saw some personal and professional qualities in him and acted in good faith to appoint him.

Jeremy has a twofold task if he is to succeed in making his mark. He must make an ally of Ian Schaffer who enjoys the support of the Chapel School parents, teachers, and students. He must also win over the principal, Cecilia Toner. He must be sensitive to the needs of Ian because it is both humane and professional to do so. If Jeremy is to be viewed as a trusted leader, he must give Ian all the help he may need. For example, Jeremy should be tolerant and supportive of Ian. He should try to involve Ian in the decision-making process of the school. He should work to give Ian more responsibility in the school as a way to motivate him. If Ian has particular interests, Jeremy should encourage him in these areas and at the same time support his overall professional development goals. Jeremy needs to increase Ian's visibility and leadership potential by suggesting that Ian serve on school committees. He may encourage Ian to chair such groups as a way to enhance his leadership skills. Depending on Ian's areas of professional interest and expertise, the assistant principal might urge him to write grants, speak at faculty confer-ences, mentor new teachers, and pursue classroom innovations. In general, Jeremy would be wise to offer his services as a career mentor for the disap-pointed Ian. These approaches by Jeremy will surely go a long way toward reducing Ian's sense of disappointment. At the same time, other faculty and parents will see Jeremy as a compassionate and sensitive leader who nurtures colleagues in their professional growth.

Jeremy also has the delicate task of convincing Cecilia that he is a capable assistant principal. How can Jeremy gain the confidence of his principal? He must carry out in a thorough and expeditious manner all the assignments she has placed on him. He cannot be late, careless, or incomplete in these tasks. He must visualize the principal's job. What are her professional and personal needs and priorities? What can he do to help in these areas? He must be reliable, informed, and offer constructive thinking to resolve school issues. He must work to develop a reputation as someone who has a keen knowledge of the school's vision and be prepared to implement that vision. He must make himself an expert in whatever professional area the principal may lack or profess little interest. Here he must complement the principal's leadership style. He should be proactive in anticipating school needs and be prepared with recommendations. He must become the person who staff, parents, and students turn to for advice and direction. He must keep Cecilia informed of his activities and his own priorities. If he is criticized, he should be dispas-sionate in accepting suggestions. He needs to be visible and available early in the morning and after school when parents and students may wish to see him. He must greet parents, students, and staff in a friendly way, and follow-up in a timely manner on their concerns. Jeremy should be his own toughest critic and hold himself accountable for all that occurs in his areas of responsibility. Jeremy's consistently loyal behavior every day will surely win him support.

Chapter Twenty

Management Stuff

Monday morning began pleasantly enough for Mary Barrington, principal of Clarksdale School. The school budget was in place. There were no incidents of poor behavior on the student bus. Student attendance was high with few latecomers. This especially pleased Mary because punctuality helped to minimize the usual disruption to classroom routines and instruction. And when Mary looked out her office window, she saw a full parking lot. In fact, a total of two teachers were absent that sunny Monday. For a faculty of forty-nine teachers, this certainly was a low number. Even better, there were competent substitute teachers available to replace the two absent teachers. Best of all, the two absent teachers had e-mailed their lesson plans.

These were all signs of progress in Mary's uphill struggle to turn Clarksdale into a more orderly and safe school. She could sit back and enjoy the relative calm as she took another sip of her usual morning tea. As the sun shone brightly into the main office, Mary was able to complete some paperwork and return phone calls. She overheard several office workers chatting excitedly about the weekend parade where the Clarksdale School Band had proudly march in their new uniforms. Mary could now turn her attention to planning for graduation exercises.

Organizing and supervising programs like graduation, student assembly celebrations, or holiday activities were the best part of Mary's job. By all accounts she was creative in her ability to rearrange schedules to find enough time in a cramped school day for practice and to supervise the myriad tasks for the big day. Seating arrangements, invitations, awards, speeches, musical selections all came under her watchful eye.

"Excuse me, Mary, you have a call from the superintendent on line one," school secretary Tricia said. "He needs to talk to you."

"Morning, Mary," murmured Jack Crawford, superintendent of the school district. A no-nonsense, facts-only administrator, he was not one to engage in small talk. After some obligatory niceties about how sharp the band looked in the parade, he wasted no time in coming to the point of his call. "Mary, I have your goals for next year but before I approve them, I see very little about your plans to demonstrate instructional leadership. Your emphasis continues to be on management stuff. Your goals statement tells me about your plans to improve school-community relations, computerize your school budget, revise your arrival and dismissal procedures, and improve student discipline. That's fine, Mary, but you know the job of principal is moving away from management needs and toward creating a learner-focused school culture. Can I get your new goals in about a week, Mary?"

The longtime principal was taken aback by the new demands imposed on her by the superintendent. Did he not realize the importance of all the "management stuff" in running a school? How much more work will this new task require of her? How can she fit instructional leadership and "management stuff" into her already ten-hour workday?

QUESTIONS

1. How would you evaluate the importance of the "management stuff" in relation to the need for instructional leadership?
2. How can a school administrator reorganize his or her school day to accommodate the new demands imposed on leaders to serve as chief learners?
3. What role do teachers play in the new leadership paradigm envisioned by the superintendent? What role does central staff play?
4. Given the expanding responsibilities assigned to administrators in schools today, there is a collateral concern about job-related stress, burnout, and early retirement. How can you maintain the necessary balance in your life to avoid suffering these occupational hazards?

COMMENTS

In the past a school administrator's managerial acumen may have been a significant part of one's effectiveness as a leader and one's evaluation report by the superintendent. In today's ever-changing world of educational leadership, however, Mary must know that successful school leaders emphasize matters of instruction, curriculum, and professional development, along with assessment of pupil progress and creating a learner-focused school culture.

They use data to guide school decision making and to review instructional progress. They know the importance of ongoing professional development to upgrade teachers' performance. The linchpin for this emphasis on instructional leadership is the principal's office.

If Mary is to succeed in freeing herself from the managerial prison that has captured many administrators, she must reshape her own work style. She must delegate decision making to her secretary and other faculty. She must improve her time management skills and learn the importance of prioritizing her workload. Mary should begin to tap into teacher talent as a means to strengthen their own sense of professionalism and to empower them as leaders too. Numerous school decisions lend themselves to teacher expertise, for example, teacher selection of textbooks, teacher determination of staff development needs, selection of new faculty, setting standards for student behavior, and writing plans for school improvement.

So how can Mary revamp her priorities and assert herself in a new role as lead learner for Clarksdale? First, Mary needs to reorder her work day. The paperwork must come last. She can begin by being out and about in the halls and in the classrooms. She needs to discuss with teachers her own high expectations for pupil achievement, professional issues, matters relating to student progress, and a curriculum innovation she has witnessed. Her visible presence in classes will communicate to faculty and students the importance placed on teaching and learning. And what should she look for when she visits classrooms? In reading class, for example, consider the following for starters:

1. Does the teacher share his or her own joy for reading?
2. Are the children reading throughout the day in *all* subject areas?
3. Do students engage classmates in what they are reading?
4. Does the teacher model reading through regular read-aloud classes as he or she tries to include different types of text?
5. Does the teacher give students ample opportunity to read in shared reading sessions, in instructional groups, and independently?
6. Does the teacher encourage students to respond critically to what they have read using student reading journals?
7. Do students read from a variety of materials with different styles, formats, and genres?

Mary must be sure to compliment teachers and students alike for their efforts to improve teaching and learning. In doing so she will encourage them to take risks in the classroom. She may want to initiate an ongoing program of professional development for faculty through intervisitations, demonstration lessons, a buddy system for inexperienced teachers, institutes and workshops by experts, and faculty meetings that emphasize curriculum and instruction.

As part of a long-term effort to improve the quality of these meetings, she should use these sessions to share with staff videotapes of live teaching situations and discuss effective practices for the classroom. With teacher permission, she may even set up a wide-screen camera and invite teachers to videotape themselves for a full lesson. They can view the tapes in the privacy of their homes.

Mary might also work with teachers to create a "critical friends group" that analyzes student work. The groups can be made more powerful if they are data-driven. Another form of teacher collaboration to improve their practice is the lesson study process whereby teams meet on a regular basis to discuss whatever learning needs students may have and develop lessons that respond to these needs. Teachers take turns teaching model lessons and evaluating one another's work until a higher level of consistency becomes the norm.

Mary should avoid the more standard forms of professional development—workshops, lectures, and district conference days—that are unpopular with teachers because they are often one-shot deals led by outside experts who will tell teachers what to do and then leave implementation to the teachers. The best kind of teacher training should incorporate a research base about good teaching practices, solve real problems, and use peer networks.

Mary can also enhance her own role as a strong leader of instruction through her attendance and participation at professional conferences, reading educational journals, joining a professional study group to analyze school trends, and visiting with principal colleagues to observe their own leadership practices in instruction.

And how can the central office use its resources to encourage school leaders like Mary to assert their new roles? Principal conferences, like faculty conferences, should revolve around issues of teaching, learning, and assessment. These conferences should adopt a case study approach in which principals present real scenarios of teachers they work with. Questions related to administration and management issues should be relegated to the end of conference time. Priority agenda items should explore the use of data in raising student achievement and the quality of instruction.

Supervisory walkthroughs offer another central office technique to help principals assume their new roles in instruction. The walkthrough focuses on professional growth and ultimately leads to more reflective conversation between central office, school administrator, and the teacher. This technique represents an occasion for the principal to lay out instructional improvement, professional development progress, and review any curricular issues that detract from obtaining school goals.

Central office leaders and school administrators can learn from one another. Their meetings could also examine videotapes of teaching and analyze what constitutes good instruction. Groups of principals might be asked to present real case studies for teachers in their schools and role play observation conferences. Principals can also critique the school improvement plans for their colleagues. Through the entire process the superintendent's office must commit itself to complete support of the new leadership role it has assigned its principals.

Chapter Twenty-one

Visiting the Classes

As Harry Garrison was driving back to the Gardens School after a conference with the superintendent, he was wondering how he could implement the latest mandate. Today's conference was on the essential need to get around the building. Harry wondered how he would be able to do that every day. He had toured the building once in a while, but it seemed to him impossible to do it often or especially every day as the superintendent insisted.

Getting out of the office to tour the building is something that is vital for all principals. Yet, with phone calls to respond to, especially when the parents call and want to talk endlessly about a child who was punched on the bus or who had a fight over the weekend, it is tough to get out of the office. These things may have nothing to do with what is happening in school, but parents want the attention and advice of the principal and often they want the principal to talk to them and solve the problem.

Then there is the paperwork to complete. The central office gets upset when paperwork comes in late. The secretary needs reports completed so she can type them and get them out. There always is another item to fill out or read and edit.

Then there are the meetings with teachers. Teachers want to let the principal know when someone is quite ill in the family or someone is getting married. In addition, they want to talk about a child who is not doing his or her homework or who is disruptive. Sometimes meeting with the teachers for curriculum or grading or new materials discussion is necessary but time consuming, especially when there are many grades involved.

It seems impossible to get out of the office to visit all the classes. Harry Garrison saw one of the teachers in the office who was always coming up with great ideas and whom he knew he could talk to. She said, "Do what you frequently do. Ask all the constituencies for ideas."

Harry met with the active parents and the teachers' consultative committee and they came up with a number of ways to get him out of the office so he could be visible throughout the building on a daily basis. Here are some of the suggestions:

1. The teachers would ask, "Please come to my room today. The students did something they want to demonstrate for you."
2. The secretary would keep an alarm clock on the desk. If he did not get out of the office by the time the alarm went off, he left when that alarm rang.
3. Children knocked on his door or wrote notes inviting him to the room to see innovative lessons and activities.
4. He was invited to team teach or teach a lesson by himself on topics he loved.
5. Someone suggested he deliver packages or video equipment to get around the building.
6. He talked to children about their achievements and progress and they would encourage him to come to their rooms and see more wonderful things they did.

The end result was that Harry got to really know the students, see how he could support the teachers, and let everyone know that he was there to help in every way possible. A good school became better!

QUESTIONS

1. Was it a good idea to consult the constituencies? Explain.
2. What makes visibility so important?
3. What impressions do teachers and parents have of principals who sit in their offices all day?

COMMENTS

Since the school improvement movement of the 1970s, it has been common practice for principals to consult various constituencies. With regard to a wide range of issues, principals are aware that they do not have all the answers and others may share thoughtful, accurate, and timely solutions to complex problems. Allowing others to share opinions about dilemmas enables principals to get answers to problems that may perplex them but not someone else. Time is saved and problems solved when principals seek help with day-to-day concerns.

Walkthroughs send signals to the teachers that the principal is supportive. He or she wants to know what issues the teachers are facing. The principal can then take action to support the teachers with discipline, curriculum implementation, and strategies that are not working. When a principal visits the rooms on a regular basis, the principal is making a statement that he or she wants to be involved and wants to be part of the improvement process. The principal's actions make this statement: "I care and I am willing to do my part to be supportive and involved." Teachers' morale is raised because they know the principal is a partner in this very important work that is being done to educate the youngsters. Sometimes new goals or new programs are instituted early in the year and principals can see firsthand how things are working. Are the goals being advanced? Are the new materials functioning as superb vehicles for instruction? Also new plans and strategies may have been planned early in the year and when the principal visits the rooms, he or she can see if they are effective.

Few may say it, but parents, teachers, office staff, and everyone who knows that the principal spends much too much time in the office thinks the principal is not doing the most effective job. The impression talked about behind the principal's back is that too much time is spent on paperwork or personal business or just not caring about what is transpiring throughout the building. Unfortunately, if people do not see the leader circulating and being a hands-on person, an impression develops in which the principal is thought of as not caring and too uninvolved.

Chapter Twenty-two

Culture Shock

Lee Wells loved all the years he had spent as an inner-city school principal. Despite the many challenges that are associated with a high poverty school, Lee was proud of his school. His record was one of leadership and achievement. Lee's annual performance evaluations were always superior. Pupil achievement was on the upswing, the community had come to support the school, and the staff earned numerous honors for their sense of professionalism. On Friday afternoons at the end of many long weeks, Lee commented to colleagues and friends, "I can't wait 'til Monday." Such was his dedication to his job. His enthusiasm was contagious as many teachers worked side by side with him to build a better school. The faculty seemed to enjoy their work as much as Lee enjoyed his job.

After several years, Lee began to feel tired. Lacking his earlier enthusiasm that had nourished him for many years as principal, Lee sought another principalship in a quiet, more affluent school district in another metropolitan area. He worked hard to get the position that he regarded as almost semiretirement. This was in comparison to his previous six years as Humanities School principal with over 80 percent of the one thousand students receiving free lunch.

Lee's new job was markedly different from his previous administrative positions. The new school, Vine Street School, was located in a town with a high socioeconomic population and, with some exceptions, a record of strong pupil achievement and parent involvement. It was these exceptions, however, that concerned the school community. With a high school tax, parents demanded more of the schools. The Board of Education and its superintendent, Albert Carlton, heard the parent complaints and resolved to shake the schools of their casual attitude toward the children who were not learning. They were equally determined to reject any general acceptance of the status quo. A first step was to encourage hiring of administrators from outside the district in the belief the outsiders would be more willing to engage the parents and teachers in a change process.

Lee was among the new cadre of administrators and teachers hired under the new selection plan. Lee's honeymoon period did not last long, however, as many of his ideas and practices were immediately challenged. For example, his practice of visiting classrooms every day to provide support for teachers and observe student progress was interpreted as checking up on the teachers. It was obvious to Lee that no supervisor in the past had visited the classes on any consistent basis. One teacher complained at a faculty meeting, "The principal's daily visits compromise the autonomy of the classroom teachers."

On another occasion, Lee tried to organize a student council. Parents and students were enthusiastic but faculty reaction was mixed, at best. At a planning meeting a teacher acidly noted that council elections would set up unnecessary student rivalries, jealousies, competition, and damage the "fragile egos" of children who might run and lose the election.

Confronted with opposition to many of his proposals, Lee sought counsel from the superintendent who respected his initiatives and ideas for change. The superintendent told his anxious principal he had heard from several teachers who complained that he was ignorant of the school's traditions and culture. Lee was too quick to institute change, complained the teachers. They wanted him to slow the pace of his change plan. The superintendent also told him that he had heard from parents about his dedication and commitment to long overdue change. He advised Lee to continue on the road to change.

Although a cadre of young teachers supported their principal, a powerful bloc of senior teachers undermined his efforts. After several months of hard work with little progress, Lee realized that the change plan had again stalled.

He decided to discuss his concerns with the superintendent over lunch. As they sat down to enjoy a rare duty-free lunch out of the school, Lee unburdened himself once more to Albert. In his heart Lee believed the school had enormous potential for excellence. He talked excitedly about the change efforts he was overseeing in curriculum, technology applications in the classes, teacher training, and in assuring parents of a greater role in school decision making. This time Lee sensed that Albert was vague and noncommittal in his support for Lee's initiatives. Sipping on a cup of coffee, the superintendent explained, "Lee, you know how slow change comes. Around here change moves as fast as a glacier. In this town the principal is like the corpse at a funeral. His presence is necessary for the event to occur but to do otherwise would be startling." Shocked, Lee considered quitting his job as principal if the superintendent could not support him.

QUESTIONS

1. Should Lee resign his position?
2. What could Lee have done differently to gain support from the teachers?
3. How can Lee help his staff cope with the changes he seeks to implement?
4. In his efforts to measure support for change, what are some signs Lee should notice? Conversely, what are some signs of resistance he should be aware of?

COMMENTS

First, it would be premature for Lee to consider resigning his position. The issues that he finds himself facing—change, conflict, faculty involvement, questionable superintendent support—are typical issues that many administrators must address. Lee needs to see his new principalship as a positive growth opportunity that will increase his leadership skills if he can successfully navigate his way through the dilemmas posed in this case.

In planning to institute changes at the Vine Street School, Lee should not think he can easily replicate the success he enjoyed at the Humanities School. Each school possesses its own traditions, values, culture, and willingness to accept change. What may have been successful at Humanities may not be appropriate for the Vine Street School. Change is specific to each school and is unique to each school situation. There is no universal model of school reform that will work in all settings. Change is too complex a variable to reduce to a single recipe.

Lee is seeking to alter some deep-rooted beliefs of the Vine Street faculty, but he has not considered the impact these changes may have on the people who stand to be most affected by the new ideas he brings. In this case the faculty stands to undergo the most change. Lee needs to maintain the high level of achievement by maintaining stable operations while simultaneously working to institute the innovations he envisions for the school.

Faculty resistance to Lee's ideas is a serious obstacle to his plans for change. This need not be a fatal obstacle, however. His first strategy might be to open a dialogue with staff. After orienting staff to his plans for change and the rationale behind his ideas, Lee may want to create an advisory team to guide the changes. Members of the team should be representative of all ages and philosophies. Special care should be given to selecting and valuing the input of senior faculty. This approach will increase participation and minimize resistance.

Before Lee tackles the substance of his changes, he must address the change process by working to promote a school culture open to change. He can plant the seeds of success by actually slowing down the pace of the changes he plans to institute. Although this may appear to be contradictory at first glance, Lee's strategy should be to lessen the resistance by generating enthusiasm for change.

So how can Lee minimize faculty resistance? The following approaches might be useful as he seeks to create a dialogue and openness to change:

1. A collaborative leadership style
2. Support for faculty initiatives
3. Tolerance of differences
4. A nonjudgmental attitude
5. Sensitivity for faculty feelings and values
6. A win-win philosophy about conflict

In adopting these approaches, Lee is building a trust relationship with the faculty. It is clear that in any change situation, trust is a more potent tool than power or coercion. He needs to communicate with individual staff members, small groups, and faculty leaders. Given the resistance on the part of the teachers, Lee must involve them in the process and make it comfortable for them to express their reservations in an open atmosphere. The Vine Street School staff is a competent and professional group, and Lee would be well advised to work with them in a participatory manner. If he is to be successful in his plans, he must secure their commitment.

So how can Lee help his staff cope with the changes he seeks? Lee must be flexible in the direction he gives. He should be willing to modify his methods. He should identify and support those directly involved in implementing the new ideas. He must maintain regular communication with those responsible for the new order he wants to create. He must listen to their concerns, mediate the inevitable conflicts that will surface, avoid scapegoating, build faculty confidence, and avoid any tendency to revert to a top-down management plan.

How will Lee know the staff is responding to the changes? If teachers assume the initiative in planning, display a sense of humor throughout the process, are willing to admit errors, suggest alternatives, and commit to spending additional time, Lee will know the faculty is at least open to change. He must continue to support their efforts.

On the other hand, any of the following indicators should be a warning to Lee to slow down the pace of change and adjust accordingly:

1. Continued apathy
2. Procrastination
3. Subtle sabotage
4. Lack of faculty willingness to participate

5. Open conflict within the faculty

Any change process implies the need for risk-taking on the part of participants. Although educators are notoriously reluctant to embrace risks, Lee
must make it clear that it is perfectly fine to make mistakes and try new
ideas. How can Lee support faculty in their willingness to accept risks? He
must help them understand that failure is okay, that different opinions should
be respected, that communication is key to change, and major decisions are
to be made in a collaborative manner. Lee must also reward their risk-taking
by giving recognition, professional development, additional resources, and
even promotional opportunities to those who participate in the change process. Most of all, he must compliment faculty for their time and effort to
make the Vine Street School a better place not only for themselves but also
for students and parents as well.

Chapter Twenty-three

The BMW Teacher

Even before he reported for his first day as principal of the Kent School, Barry Pennisi sensed that Denise Simmons, a senior teacher, would challenge him. When it was announced that he would be selected as principal, Denise found his phone number listed in the phonebook. Barry's phone rang at dinner. Denise wasted little time in extending good wishes. Instead she harangued him over the phone as she complained about "the influx of new kids who ruined our school, their parents who always defend their kids, and the other teachers who can't handle the kids." She advised Barry as to which teachers he could trust and those to be wary of. She sprinkled her complaints with a slew of racial and religious epithets.

Lest anyone be spared her diatribe, Denise further complained about the teachers' union that "protects those sorry teachers" and about the central office that "never does anything for Kent but to dump the worst teachers and the worst students on the school." Not even the new principal escaped her wrath. She challenged his credentials. "And you, Mr. Pennisi, what experience do you have to be principal? You are the third principal since last year. Some teachers are taking bets you will not last either." As she continued her litany of complaints against the kids, their parents, the teachers, and sundry other groups, Barry suddenly lost his appetite. It was to be the first of many dinnertime interruptions.

When Barry took a personal day to attend the funeral of his uncle, Denise wrote an anonymous letter to the superintendent complaining that Barry was not attending any funeral but was taking off on a long weekend. Barry began to see Denise as one of those BMW teachers that his professor talked about when he was studying to be a principal. According to his professor, a BMW teacher is one who blames, moans, and whines. Yes, that was Denise. He also recalled his professor's advice to deal with the BMW teachers quickly or they would infect the entire organization with their negativity.

Another time, while making his rounds and visiting teachers in the classrooms, Barry noticed that nearly all the doors to the classrooms were locked. When he reminded teachers the doors should be unlocked as a matter of policy, they retorted, "But Denise has a free period now and may scold us as well as the kids if she knows she can get into our rooms."

On another occasion, Barry received a letter from the town mental health clinic informing him that the staff psychiatrist was treating several students for severe phobia. Their teacher? Denise Simmons. When Barry arranged a meeting to talk with Denise about the extreme measures she used in her classroom, Denise came to the meeting accompanied by several parents who supported her discipline approach as "necessary for a safe class." Parents also praised Denise for her knowledge of curriculum, her ability to respond to the diverse learning needs of students, and the learning atmosphere in her class that produced excellent student achievement. Denise readily admits she experiences a great sense of fulfillment and pride in teaching students to appreciate literature.

One of Barry's first strategies was to open a dialogue with Denise. He encouraged her to share her concerns with him. Barry believed in the theory that it is good to keep your friends close but your enemies closer. He tried conciliation as an approach to deal with her anger. After each ranting episode, Barry would try to calm her, "Thank you for sharing your concerns. I look forward to working with you." Communication and pleasantries did not assuage Denise. She interpreted the principal's kindness as weakness and continued to undermine him and the school.

QUESTIONS

1. What are some other effective approaches to deal with Denise?
2. Should a principal's phone number be listed in the telephone directory?
3. When Barry realized he was being undermined, what strategies should he have adopted in response?
4. Should Barry have allowed the parents who supported Denise to remain in his meeting with her?
5. What resources are available to help Barry resolve his difficulties with Denise?

COMMENTS

Barry has a variety of options at his disposal. He can transfer the children who are undergoing medical treatment for school phobia to other classes. He can also remove his phone number from the phone directory and get an unlisted number. Will these ideas solve Barry's difficulty? Hardly.

Barry must develop a fuller plan to address the BMW teacher. He needs to ask himself several questions: Is this issue worth his time and effort? What would be the consequences if Barry did nothing in this case? Are Denise's actions part of an overall pattern of unprofessional conduct or are they isolated examples? Is Denise aware of the controversy she has created within the school? How did previous administrators deal with Denise? With what success?

Dealing with a difficult person like Denise is an unpleasant task for any principal. This may be especially so for a new principal like Barry. Should he try to isolate or ignore Denise? This approach is doubtful for several reasons. First, his attempt to avoid confrontation and conflict with Denise may inadvertently create more tension. She is like the eight-hundred-pound gorilla in the room that no one wishes to discuss but all are aware of. Barry's silence could be interpreted as consent of her actions. Second, avoidance may cause other faculty to question his leadership ability. Third, Denise's outbursts about students, parents, colleagues, and central office are ruinous to the good order of the entire school and, if ignored, can further infect the culture at Kent School.

As a senior faculty member with full job security and due process rights, Denise cannot be terminated or dismissed so easily. At the beginning of the school year, Barry must inform her in writing that improvement in interpersonal relationships will be one of the factors that will determine her final rating when the school year is concluded. This must be a major component in her performance evaluation.

The onus is on Barry to find a creative resolution to the dilemma of Denise. First, Barry must continue his efforts to improve Denise's relationships with faculty, parents, and the entire school community. This may be a tall order for Denise to achieve but Barry owes it to Denise to help her on a personal and professional level. As prickly as her personality may be, this is the essence of good leadership that will increase Barry's credibility. Barry must help her understand she must respect colleagues and children alike. Although Denise may have ridiculed his initial overtures to build a relationship with her, Barry must continue to listen to her, use her ideas, never ridicule her, and praise her for her good work in the classroom.

Assuming success in helping Denise improve her relationships, Barry can work to channel her talents into a resource to further the professional growth of less experienced teachers. He can assign her as a mentor to assist new teachers. He may also ask her to design model lessons or lead faculty conferences that relate to her areas of expertise. Denise may welcome these challenges as opportunities to demonstrate her professional skills to colleagues and provide some valuable assistance to the new principal. All of these ideas, of course, are contingent on Denise's ability and willingness to improve her interpersonal relationships with colleagues.

If Barry's best efforts to help Denise become a productive and valued teacher do not meet with success, Barry must then invoke a ladder of progressive discipline. This ladder is a series of graduated consequences meant to obtain proper compliance with Board of Education policy. The ladder may have consequences ranging from letters of discipline for one's personnel file, to suspension without pay, to transfer, to dismissal and termination of employment. Barry may also consider referring her to the employee assistance unit that every central office provides as part of the human resource function of school management.

In his efforts to address a difficult case like that of Denise, Barry should be willing to seek advice from other resources that might help him. Certainly principal colleagues, the school superintendent, the legal counsel of the Board of Education, and even her clergyman or members of Denise's family may be in a position to help Denise.

Throughout the entire process Barry must continue to document the assistance given Denise with the ultimate goal of terminating her employment if her performance impacts negatively on the school or the students.

Chapter Twenty-four

The Vision Thing

Soon after his appointment as principal of the Willis School, Ed Leary discovered some of the serious issues facing the school. Teacher morale was low. Pupil achievement was declining. Parents did not support the school, and the more sophisticated parents had gotten waivers that allowed their children to attend other schools. Discipline was so poor that the parent-teacher association offered to set up a parent patrol squad in the halls.

Teachers placed much of the responsibility for the school's problems on a changing pupil population. "These kids just don't want to learn" was a common refrain at faculty meetings and in the staff lounge. Parents, on the other hand, blamed the school's difficulties on teachers who were not understanding of the new and diverse groups of people moving into the community.

To resolve the tensions Ed convened a broad-based committee of faculty and staff, parents, and interested members of the community. Their task was to collectively develop a school vision. Ed planned a series of meetings to draft a vision that would focus on student achievement as the end result. Open discussions were held but the response was mixed. Ed tried diligently to foster faculty input into matters of school governance, for example, curriculum, promotion policies for students, selection of staff to fill two vacancies, and the school discipline plan. Teachers, though, were not sure if they really would have any meaningful role in the school's vision because, in the words of one teacher, "the previous principal also practiced shared decision-making but it was a sham. He always made the decisions and then he shared them with the teachers." Teachers also had a reluctance to share any information or concerns with the parents.

Parents, on the other hand, reacted favorably to Ed's invitation that they be part of the vision committee. They were pleased by his sense of trustworthiness and honesty. Ed tried to empower parents to have a voice in the decision-making process.

By not making decisions from the top down, but from a general appreciation for parent and faculty participation, Ed hoped to cultivate mutual dialogue on the part of the overall school community. This was his general philosophy of leadership, but given the communication gap between the parents and teachers, he was beginning to reconsider his approach to the wisdom of collaborative planning.

QUESTIONS

1. What are some reasons why the teachers were reluctant to participate with parents on the school vision committee?
2. What could Ed do to facilitate an honest exchange of ideas between faculty and parents?
3. Given the controversy surrounding collaboration between parents and faculty, if you were the principal, would you continue to encourage a shared decision-making model at Ed's school? If not, what other leadership approaches would you use to obtain your objectives?
4. Would Ed be well advised to accept the parent-teacher association's offer to set up a hall patrol squad as a means to deter discipline problems? What issues does this offer raise for Ed as school principal?

COMMENTS

Ed must not place blame on the faculty because they do not meet his professional standards. He must understand that employees in general respond to the norms and values of their environment. Here the teachers are simply responding to the negative climate that existed under his predecessor. For Ed to change the distrustful environment at Willis to one that is more open will require a great deal of time, persistence, faith, and leadership on his part.

Ed is stymied by faculty distrust of his initiatives. He should not be surprised by their reluctance to assume a leadership role in the operations of the school. Ed must now work to reverse the history of the Willis School. He should not, however, abandon his plans to develop a collaborative workplace. To do so would only intensify the dysfunctional environment that currently exists at the school.

As principal Ed's policies and decisions will play a prominent role in setting the appropriate tone for the school. His ultimate goal is to create a more professional learning environment for all of the school's constituents.

Honest professional dialogue that examines faculty values and attitudes is an essential building block for the development of this learning community. The dialogue must be based on trust that the faculty and the principal will make decisions with the best interests of students at the forefront.

Ed can influence the dialogue by the example he sets. He should work to provide time and create mechanisms to encourage honest discussions among faculty. He can start small by organizing teams of faculty members who share his goals or who may have particular expertise he can draw on. These teams may produce a ripple effect that can impact other staff members. He cannot fall into the trap of allowing the planning teams to be viewed as cliques. To avoid this trap he must communicate regularly with the entire staff. His full faculty meetings, for example, should become one-way communication forums in which he must be prepared to listen intently to faculty concerns. He must follow-up on these concerns, which is especially important if he is to build the culture of trust that will allow collaboration to flourish.

Ed might also consider the idea of having a coffee pot or a bowl of candy in his office, and invite faculty to partake. Such ideas encourage dialogue. Ed also needs to offer a sense of community for the entire school. One approach might be to organize a school-wide event that will attract faculty, parents, and students alike in a nonthreatening arena. Depending on the time of year, options might include a Back to School Night, Willis School Dinner, school picnic, school play, or a school softball or basketball game. The presence of food and entertainment at these events generally serves to lower the barriers to communication and enhance the collegial atmosphere.

At the beginning of the school year Ed should recommend to his teachers that they make an introductory call to the parents of their students. This call should be light and positive in which the teacher expresses his or her pleasure at having one's child in class. What a powerful message to parents that the teacher does care! If the adage is true that people do not care how much you know until they know you care, then Willis School teachers can earn trust with parents and students by demonstrating care with a phone call. Parents are more apt to listen to a teacher's comments about their children's progress when they already have a relationship with the teacher.

Ed should also enlist key power brokers in the school by building communication lines with the faculty representatives and with parent leaders. Once he develops a genuine communication with these groups and they with one another, the cycle of trust can grow.

The development of trust as a common framework for decision making can offer important dividends for the entire school community. Teachers would be more likely to share materials and successful teaching strategies, encourage colleagues in their professional growth, and commit to student success. They might also be more accessible to parents and receptive to parent sentiment. When Ed, the faculty, and parents trust one another, a climate of openness ensues and engagement on behalf of students is more likely. When teachers believe parents are supportive, they work together to improve the learning environment for students.

In one study of the relationship between trust and student achievement, it was found that the greater the trust between parents and teachers, the higher the level of student performance in reading and in math. This was true even when the impact of student socioeconomic status was considered (Goddard, Tschannen-Moran, and Hoy 2001). In a long-term study of schools in Chicago that were involved in school reform over a ten-year period, Bryk and Schneider (2002) found that trust was a critical determinant in predicting which schools would produce the greatest academic gains and which schools would maintain those gains. Schools that displayed greater trust produced higher student achievement that lasted longer than other schools where trust was not evident. In his campaign to develop a collaborative learning environment devoid of fault or blame, Ed may want to share this research with faculty and engage them in a dialogue on the role of trust in professional relationships.

REFERENCES

Bryk, A. S., and B. Schneider. 2002. *Trust in schools: A core resource for school improvement.* New York: Russell Sage Foundation.

Goddard, R. D., M. Tschannen-Moran, and W. K. Hoy. 2001. A multilevel examination of the distribution and effects of teacher trust in students and parents in urban elementary schools. *Elementary School Journal* 102 (1): 3–17.

Chapter Twenty-five

Serving Two Masters

Jim Wynn, principal of Temple School, was widely seen as a model school leader. As caring as he was to protect his staff from intrusion into their classroom teaching and help them in their professional growth, Jim also set high standards for himself as someone who was very task-oriented in this work. Faculty respected him because they knew he always factored in their needs and concerns as he carried out the many assignments the central office imposed on him. The superintendent, Anthony Miles, also valued Jim as a leader because he kept the superintendent's staff informed of any issues that could embarrass or hurt the district. Jim was also seen as a team player and loyal to the district. Anthony was an especially demanding superintendent who issued numerous directives to his principals. Jim was quite adept in responding to the many orders coming from the superintendent's office. Anthony appreciated Jim's efficiency in tending to district priorities.

Temple School was always highly achieving, and Jim enjoyed good relationships with faculty, parents, students, and the entire community. Jim was identified as a "comer" for a future position high up in the central administration where his many skills would come in quite handy. Indeed, he excelled in many areas of educational leadership—in initiating new curriculum, promoting a positive learning environment, resolving conflict, maintaining high staff performance, setting a "no excuses" standard of expectations, and building strong relationships with the parents and community. He had even won some significant grants to encourage innovative professional development.

In one area of administration, however, Jim was less confident. He did not understand, nor did he even try to comprehend, even the basics of school budgets. He found the entire subject to be professionally unsatisfying. To compensate for this weakness, Jim often relied on the assistant principal, Charlie Montgomery, as his budget maven and chief administrator. This relationship worked well because Charlie was expert in preparing and modifying the school budget and somehow always pulling a fiscal trick out of his hat to find money for some new program. Charlie also was a master at organizing the school schedule. Most important, Charlie used his technological knowhow to create spreadsheets that followed the nuances of the budget and the school schedules. Charlie's skills in these areas made him invaluable to his principal who even volunteered Charlie's services to assist administrators in other schools in their efforts to devise responsible budgets and student-friendly schedules. These opportunities to share his expertise helped Charlie increase his own visibility throughout the school district. This was just one of many ways that Jim promoted his staff and shared their talents with other schools. With helpful ways like this it was no wonder that Temple School had earned for itself the unofficial motto of "WIN WITH WYNN."

When the superintendent needed a school-by-school review of budgetary appropriations in anticipation of a Board of Education demand for a shift in spending from administration to more services for special needs children, he called each principal to schedule a presentation before the Board of Education. Jim's school was scheduled for April 1, six weeks away. He told Charlie to put the date on his calendar as both would speak before the Board of Education.

A few days before the budget meeting, Jim asked Charlie to brief him on the presentation. Charlie responded, "I can't make the meeting." After a long pause and a quizzical look on his face, Jim asked, "Is this an April Fool's joke? Well, it's not funny! You know how much I am counting on you as the budget maven." Charlie proceeded to tell his boss that his son, Charles Jr., had been selected as starting pitcher for the high school all-star baseball game scheduled for April 1. A single father whose wife had died in a car accident a year ago, Charlie felt he could not disappoint his only son. "How come you never told me?" asked Jim. "I need you at that meeting. I was really counting on you."

Clearly embarrassed, Charlie blurted out, "I forgot and when I did remember, I was afraid to tell you. I thought the Board might change the date. I know you are disappointed in me, and I am sorry. I just can't disappoint my son. Please don't ask me to, Jim."

QUESTIONS

1. Should Jim order his assistant principal to attend the budget meeting of the Board of Education?
2. What are the benefits and drawbacks if Jim should direct Charlie to attend the meeting?

3. How would Jim's decision affect his relationship with his assistant principal and with the superintendent?
4. What alternatives can you suggest to resolve Jim's dilemma?
5. Discuss Jim's leadership style in relation to the faculty, to Charlie, and Anthony.

COMMENTS

Jim exudes all the characteristics of a good leader. He is people-oriented and task-oriented. He knows the value of relationships and is also focused on the assignments before him as principal. He is masterful in his ability to support his faculty and to work with a demanding boss like Anthony. Where he may have some deficiency in terms of his limited knowledge of budget and administration, Jim is smart enough to hire Charlie Montgomery as his assistant principal. In doing so Jim is practicing the technique of complementary supervision, that is, identifying his own leadership shortcomings and then hiring someone who can fill in the areas of responsibility and expertise that he may lack.

In this case study, Jim's dilemma is that he is serving two masters, namely, his support for staff and his support for his superintendent. Which is more important? Jim must decide if he should be sensitive to his assistant principal or help Charlie understand that the needs of the organization take priority over personal matters. The careers of both Jim and Charlie could well be on the line in this instance.

The obvious solution for Jim is simply to inform Charlie that his work and his career come before any family concerns. "Sorry, Charlie, but I am your supervisor. Don't disappoint me or the superintendent or the Board of Education," would seem a realistic response to Charlie.

But is it realistic? Are there alternatives? Ideally, Jim could seek a postponement of his school's presentation to the Board of Education. Jim could ask Charlie to tutor another staff member who has shown skill and a willingness to deal with budget issues. He could also easily wish Charlie good luck and best wishes in the all-star game, and then go it himself with a little tutoring from Charlie. In covering for Charlie, Jim would be demonstrating the law of support. Simply stated, the law holds that if a leader wants a subordinate to commit to the success of the leader and the success of the organization, then the leader must support the subordinate in his personal needs, professional growth, or whatever else is important to the success and satisfaction of the subordinate. In other words, one must give loyalty to get loyalty.

Jim could excuse Charlie from the meeting thereby respecting Charlie's family obligation. Charlie, in turn, needs to be willing and available to tutor his boss or a colleague in a crash course of budgeting. This is a win-win for Jim and for Charlie.

Chapter Twenty-six

The Game Plan

The Fenton School had long been recognized as a place of learning for its students. The longtime principal Alice Bellamy had worked for many years to recruit a top-notch staff. She was diligent in her pursuit of grant opportunities to encourage new approaches to instruction. By all accounts she was quite adept at this task. One successful grant, Bits and Bytes, resulted in a $25,000 venture that integrated technology with the teaching of a new math and science curriculum. Another successful grant, Tombstones to Texts, awarded the school several thousand dollars to study local history through an exploration of the town cemetery.

Alice was equally persistent in her desire to promote professional development for faculty. This became a standard strategy in her plan to enhance the learning culture at Fenton. The end result for all was consistently high student achievement, a stable faculty, and a supportive parent-teacher association. Alice's tenure as principal earned her a performance bonus for three consecutive years. There was, however, no way to calculate the enormous professional and personal satisfaction she derived from serving as Fenton's principal.

On the advice of her accountant, but against her own better judgment, Alice decided to retire. She left a legacy of staff professionalism and a record of student success. Her school had earned the distinction of being the number-one school in the district and the entire metropolitan area. Faculty had won numerous accolades for excellence in teaching. Parents competed vigorously to get their children admitted to Fenton. The local colleges used the school as a laboratory for its future teachers.

After Alice's retirement, the Board of Education appointed Mike Grover as the new principal. Mike was a recent graduate of the Principal's Leadership Institute initiated by a coalition of school districts to address the shortage of qualified and competent principals. After a year of serving full time as an apprentice to another school principal, he felt ready to take on his own school. Mike had learned a variety of skills to make him, as he told faculty, ready to "hit the ground running." The Leadership Institute had taught him the latest techniques in effective school leadership, innovative theories of instruction, time management skills, and how to build a community of learners.

Mike carved out an ambitious improvement plan for Fenton School. He visited classes daily, sometimes twice. As a recognized expert in curriculum, he felt he had much to offer teachers in the way of improving their repertoire of instructional strategies. He would be the first to arrive in the morning and the last to leave at night. Parents and staff, as they drove through the town, could see his office from the main road. They often commented that the lights in his office were on well after dark. Mike estimated that he put in a solid twelve-hour workday. He was proud of the "tight ship" he was running. Cognizant of the research about innovative pedagogical practices, he imposed his own approach to curriculum and teaching. He directed that all teachers maintain time-on-task and resist any tendency toward distractions or tangential classroom discussions. He required uniforms for students and better dress for teachers. "Clothes maketh the man," he liked to say. "Besides if we are to be treated as professionals, then we must dress the part."

Mike did not suffer fools quietly. He had no time for small talk with teachers and found chatting with faculty and parents "nonproductive." When teachers offered their recommendations to improve school planning, Mike would respond, "Just stick to the game plan. It worked for me at the institute. Stay the course." When parents tried to schedule appointments to discuss the progress of their children, he often did not return messages until the second or third call. He instructed parents to follow the chain of command by contacting teachers before calling him about pupil concerns.

QUESTIONS

1. Assess the effectiveness of Mike's entry plan as the new principal of the Fenton School.
2. What can Mike do to improve his own performance as principal and the performance of the school?
3. What role can Alice Bellamy play in Mike's orientation to the Fenton School? Give specific suggestions.
4. What are some reasons that Mike might have adopted the approach he did as the new principal?

COMMENTS

Mike has inherited an obviously achieving school bequeathed to him by the outgoing principal Alice Bellamy. The learning environment at Fenton does not require immediate or abrupt changes in personnel or curriculum. If Mike is to succeed as principal, he must understand that effective leadership requires attention to task and attention to people. He is certainly task-oriented but he must reassess his game plan. His expertise as a leader of curriculum and instruction, while commendable, will not serve him well because he runs the risk of alienating faculty, parents, and students alike. Effective administrators encourage faculty participation in the school decision-making process. They know how to work with and through their school community to accomplish their goals. For Mike to impose any quick change or new policies without consultation or collaboration with key constituent groups could well be counterproductive and launch him into a career-ending situation. If he persists in his top-down, command-and-control leadership style, he may encounter apathy at best and outright resistance at worst. Teachers may no longer share best pedagogical practices. The teachers' association may complain bitterly about his failure to recognize teacher talents. Parents themselves may voice their misgivings and refrain from continued cooperation with the school. Student achievement may suffer as well in this atmosphere of distrust.

A more relationship-oriented leadership style that emphasizes communication and interpersonal skills will be more effective in helping him achieve his vision. Mike would be better advised to meet with the various school constituencies to introduce himself as the new school head. His agenda should be simple and focus on building the trust and support of the school community. His initial moves might include a faculty conference, parent-teacher association meeting, and a student assembly commending them on their long record of success. He should use these forums to celebrate the past year's accomplishments and extend ample credit to faculty, parents, and the student body. He should ask them all for their ideas to build on the Fenton record of achievement. He should be commended for his visibility about the school, but he should use this strategy as a way to express support for teachers and to display sensitivity to the needs of classroom teachers. He should continue to praise their efforts and provide all the support he can.

If he pursues these ideas, he will build the positive relationships and trust he will need to enhance Fenton's already superior performance. He should view Alice Bellamy as a mentor who could educate him about the school's own values and traditions. He can use the trust and relationships he builds to work with the entire school family to lay out plans for future improvement. If he is to succeed, he must build on the reservoir of talent and achievement at

Fenton. Mike must work with the faculty and parents to sustain the school's admirable record. He can do this by meeting individually and in small groups with teachers and with parents so he can build the necessary dialogue to promote Fenton.

Chapter Twenty-seven

Is Bernie Burning Out?

"I can't wait 'til Monday" was the usual refrain that Bernie Giles uttered every Friday afternoon. Bernie clearly relished his position as principal of Lawrenceville Day School. He liked to describe school leadership as "a calling, not a job." When he would do periodic lectures at local colleges on the life of an administrator, Bernie always emphasized the positive aspects of being a principal: the chance to build a superior, well-trained faculty and staff; the challenge of providing for the academic and social needs of students with "great potential to excel"; the task of securing sufficient support and resources to help teachers and students achieve to their fullest; the need to establish ongoing partnerships with parents and community agencies. He often added, "I like the fast-paced nature of school administration. My job is so varied and interesting that I do not have time to be bored. The adrenaline rush propels me every day. When I resolve a problem, it is intensely satisfying." Where some of his colleagues might describe a principal's job as nothing but "headaches and problems sprinkled with crises," Bernie saw the job as an opportunity that challenged his own intellectual and physical stamina. "One principal's crisis is another principal's opportunity" was another adage he often mentioned as he went about his daily rounds.

Bernie seemed destined for greater success as an educational leader. Under his direction as principal of Lawrenceville, academic achievement on the part of students soared. Faculty routinely won professional accolades for excellence in teaching. He pursued innovative ideas to promote parent involvement. He regularly held parent-teacher association meetings in the community to accommodate working parents who could not travel at night by public transportation to the school. As a result of the record he established as principal, Bernie was recognized as Principal of the Year. His hard work and commitment to the Lawrenceville community were yielding benefits to

117

the school and to his own career. Superintendent Jane Sobel viewed him as a "comer."

Bernie enjoyed the challenges of the job and its need for creativity, energy, administrative skill, sensitivity, and healthy doses of passion. It was the latter quality he especially needed to confront the apathy and sometimes blatant resistance from those who did not share his vision or his enthusiasm for education.

The pressure began to take its toll on Bernie after five years at the helm of a large school with nearly one thousand students. Night meetings and weekend work caused him to neglect his family responsibilities. On more than a few occasions Bernie missed his daughter Allison's dance recitals and his son Adam's Little League baseball games—much to the consternation of his wife, Sally. Their social life began to suffer because he was generally too tired after the usual ten-hour workday. Increasingly Bernie was postponing or eliminating completely from his schedule some daily "down time" he knew he needed. His lunch was sandwiched between meetings and phone calls. His desire for physical exercise was something "I'll do tomorrow." He even forgot an important medical appointment that took him so long to obtain.

Other consequences of work-related stress manifested themselves. His decisions became hasty and he had to reverse himself on numerous occasions. Collaboration and consultation with faculty became less frequent. Perhaps feelings of inadequacy emerged. Relationships with staff and parents became frayed. He became less visible around the school. The professional journals he loved to read now began to pile up unread. He began to take days off to replenish his waning energy. When he and Sally took a much-needed vacation, Bernie brought along faculty evaluations reports. He felt "stuck" in a job that was weighing on him more and more.

During the drive home from work late one evening, Bernie pondered, "What happened? Where did I go wrong? How do I regroup? What do I do next?"

QUESTIONS

1. What are some positive aspects that draw you to school leadership?
2. What is your personal plan to maintain necessary balance in your life to help you succeed as a school administrator?
3. What advice do you have for Bernie as he confronts his job situation?

COMMENTS

Job-related stress is a common characteristic of any leadership position. Individuals like Bernie who care deeply about their work and succeeding in their careers are often the most likely to face stress and burnout. Those prone to this condition are generally high achievers who demand a great deal of themselves and others. The question then is not so much how to avoid job stress but how to manage it in a positive way.

Stress is not by itself a completely negative force. On the contrary, some degree of stress motivates individuals to higher performance and greater job productivity. The complexity of challenging work assignments excites many administrators and summons up innate talents that may previously lay dormant. That in itself produces greater personal and professional satisfaction.

Is the situation hopeless for Bernie? Is he burned out? A variety of suggestions are in order for Bernie and countless other school executives. A first step is to utilize school resources by tapping into staff talents. Leave others to make decisions on their own without his constant input. Train office staff to deflect routine phone calls, upset parents, and anxious staff. He must be clear about work standards and recognize good performance. And he must not micromanage the work of office staff.

Bernie must learn how to manage his time in ways that will conserve his energy. For example, he must prioritize work assignments, learn to say no, and use technology as a labor-saving aid. Using e-mail, a Palm Pilot, or a Blackberry can save him time and effort. Where possible, send e-mails and avoid burdensome meetings. He should surround himself with good advisers whom he trusts. He must find the time to exercise by budgeting that aspect into his daily schedule. Exercise will not only improve his physical and emotional well-being, it will improve his productivity and help him cope better.

Bernie may want to network with principal colleagues because they provide another support group to share similar problems. But he also needs to spend time with friends outside education because this offers a different perspective on work. And certainly Bernie must find time to relax with hobbies and use humor too. A Norwegian proverb has particular advice for Bernie: "He who laughs, lasts." A sense of humor, which many might take for granted, actually serves as a powerful coping mechanism and has strong therapeutic value by increasing oxygen to the blood, causing a drop in blood pressure and producing more endorphins. The end result is a general lowering of tension. Apologize where appropriate. People will respect his integrity.

Being a principal is often described as a juggling act that requires an administrator to manage multiple tasks simultaneously, but this only leads to a feeling of being overwhelmed. Instead, what may work for Bernie is to stay focused on one issue at a time, however briefly it may be. Resolve that issue and move on to the next. Close the door to avoid unnecessary interruption. Bernie must retrain himself not to overreact to problems. He must learn to defuse angry people and improve his skills in resolving conflict.

Through an honest assessment of his job situation, Bernie can certainly rejuvenate himself. He can seek new professional challenges like mentoring future administrators, making presentations at professional conferences, writing articles for publication in journals, pursuing another graduate degree, initiating new programs. A paid sabbatical may be in order. These strategies can be used to revive Bernie's professional career.

Chapter Twenty-eight

But Can She Teach?

With so many foreign students attending schools in the United States, bilingual programs have proliferated. As a result, two schools of thought have developed. One group believes strongly that youngsters should maintain their former language, instill pride in their homeland, and continue that culture within the child. The other group believes in its own position that contrasts markedly with the first group. This group advocates that foreign youngsters be assimilated as soon as possible through immersion experiences in English.

When Bill Pines, principal of the Jose Marti School, learned his superintendent ordered him to start a bilingual program for incoming kindergarten children, he found an extraordinary teacher for that program. She spoke Spanish and presented herself well in terms of pedagogical knowledge as well as displaying a deep and sincere concern for children. Mrs. Lopez was a wonderful person and the teaching staff, office staff, and parents quickly found her to be cordial and very serious about her work. Most of all, the children found her to be caring and very nurturing.

Mrs. Lopez came in early and met with any child who came to school early. She tutored them, gave them work and fun activities, and even gave them snacks. At lunchtime, any child having problems could come to the room and talk to her or get extra help. She did the same thing during her preparation periods. No principal could ask for more than the very dedicated Mrs. Lopez.

When Bill visited the room often, he found that the room was decorated beautifully with magnificent posters and lovely artwork done by the children. Almost every Latin American and Caribbean country was reflected in the bulletin boards and wall posters. He noticed the children were very happy and that they were actively engaged in work. He was delighted with the interaction between Mrs. Lopez and students. She made every student feel welcome and comfortable. They, in turn, felt wanted there, worthy, and very special.

One concern that troubled Bill each time he visited Mrs. Lopez's class was that she frequently turned the conversation to Spanish. Sometimes it would be to give directions or to get a child started in an activity. Sometimes it was only a friendly conversation. Bill thought that perhaps this was a part of the standard curriculum. Since Mrs. Lopez was so devoted and task-oriented, he did not call her into the office, criticize her, or ask her to change her style, methods, and approaches. In actuality, he was so happy to have such a wonderful teacher who prepared thoroughly and had such wonderful relationships with the students and the parents.

In May a very surprising thing occurred. Several Hispanic parents who had children assigned to the bilingual class in the coming fall came to talk to Bill. They pleaded with him not to place their children in the bilingual class. Bill was shocked! After talking to them for a while, he learned that they were upset because they had spoken to their friends who had children in this year's class. The students were happy and loved the class, the lessons, and the teacher. They did not, however, learn very much English.

Needless to say, the parents bombarded the central office about their desire for a combination of immersion and English as a second language class. The district office told Bill that the bilingual program would not be a part of his school anymore.

In October, Bill met with the teachers who were receiving bilingual students. He asked them to discuss the levels of the children in their classes. He found another surprise. Each teacher said that for the most part the students entered the grade with sufficient skills, except for the bilingual youngsters. Each and every one of the teachers said that the former bilingual students were by far the least ready.

QUESTIONS

1. Why might Mrs. Lopez's students be the least ready for the next grade?
2. Should Bill have called Mrs. Lopez into his office to discuss the overuse of Spanish? Explain.
3. How do you feel about bilingual education? Explain. In your opinion, what approach to bilingual education represents the best course to follow?

COMMENTS

Ideally, teachers of bilingual classes will display respect for the culture and language of the children and thoroughly teach all the necessary and appropriate academics. Foreign students need to acquire all the skills in school that will enable them to eventually succeed in the adult working world. If they are limited by the language in America, they will be quite limited in what they can earn as adults. In some cases a bilingual teacher may go overboard in terms of speaking to the students in their native language as well as recognizing their culture and holidays. It is vital that there be substantive emphases on reading, math, writing, and other academic skills in English each and every day in the bilingual class. It is an injustice to the students to place culture and the original language as the overriding aspect of the school day. There needs to be substantive time for teaching and learning English and acquiring the important concepts and skills necessary for success in the next grade in school.

Bill should have discussed her instruction plan, or lack of academic instruction, with Mrs. Lopez. He should have told her she needed to teach the same reading, math, and writing when other teachers in that grade were teaching them. He should have asked her to explain why she was spending so much time on culture and not enough on teaching the essentials needed for the next grade. He also should have discussed the overuse of the children's original language. There should have been a dialogue where Bill told her that she must teach the class to learn English so that the pupils can use it in the regular classes at some future date and that she would be preparing them for the world outside the classroom. Bill was irresponsible not to intervene. He should have been assertive so that the students would be able to start the next year with the academic skills they needed and not be so far behind.

One could find research to advocate or criticize bilingual education. One way to look at this issue is to insist that when the children are in a bilingual environment there should be a rigorous implementation of the curriculum in which the basics are taught and there is some emphasis on teaching English. When bilingual education overemphasizes the culture and the natural language, it is doing a disservice to the youngsters. In the short term, it may seem that there is much respect for the children. In the long run it is very destructive not to have a rigorous academic program. The youngsters will need English to eventually succeed educationally and financially in the United States. It is vital that each child learn to speak, read, and write English fluently and with mastery.

Whether it is immersion or bilingual education all students in America must learn English. When a program teaches English, reading, writing, listening, and speaking thoroughly and effectively, that program is a success.

Chapter Twenty-nine

A Community of Teachers

Principals can effectively plan and implement needed changes when they involve the staff fully from the beginning through the evaluation process. The teachers involved can help find the best way to introduce the changes to the rest of the staff. They can provide ideas that would make the plan workable as well as make it effective to achieve the goals of the principal. Committed staff members can assist with the presentation process and help get the staff to take ownership of the change. As a result, the principal gains trust, respect, and loyalty from the staff.

Donna Harrington, principal of the Farm View School, scheduled a meeting with five of the most respected teachers in the building. Donna sent the committee members her agenda two days in advance and asked if they had any agenda items for the meeting. She indicated that she wanted to change the way the standard observations had been conducted in the past. She wanted teachers to be more involved in their own observations and to be more reflective about what they were teaching.

She started the meeting by saying she did not want to add burdens to the already overburdened staff. The representatives gave a sigh of relief. Donna said she had been the principal at the school for fifteen years and felt the staff deserved more leeway with keeping up with current ideas in education. She said she had enormous confidence in her teachers and felt that they were quite capable of looking at themselves in an objective manner in order to continually improve their teaching as outstanding educators always do.

Faculty leader Harold Robinson said he would be willing to work out the specifics with the staff if he had the opportunity to see what they felt they needed to improve. He realized that several staff members had been teaching a long time and they did not believe they needed to make any changes to improve.

Celeste Parrish said that she felt many staff members would be open to the change if they could plan them or at least be on committees to make the changes.

Donna explained that some of the staff members have been asking about engaging interclass visits and even making suggestions to each other.

"But the recommendations would have to be confidential among the two or three people who were observing each other. Also, it is important that we use a word like professional support, not observation, or anything that could be meant to mean evaluation," added Harold Robinson.

Donna immediately agreed.

Jack Haroldson suggested that the teachers meet by grade. Afterward they could meet by grade with Donna, and she agreed to this.

Carlos Rodriguez suggested that this be implemented slowly after much consideration by all parties. "Perhaps this year could be used to flesh out the details and then implement the new observation process next year," he stated.

Donna acquiesced. She said she would like updates from the grades when they met with her in the monthly grade meetings. Everyone agreed.

Donna also told the committee that she had gotten approval for the modification from the superintendent and his assistants. They thought it was in line with current research.

A month later, Donna met with the teachers at the grade meetings. The prekindergarten, kindergarten, and first-grade teachers shared their plan, which Donna thought was outstanding. Two or three teachers were going to observe a teacher instruct the class and then provide practical suggestions. They were going to point out exemplary practices too.

The second-grade and fourth- and fifth-grade teachers had set up a satisfactory plan. They were going to watch each other teach and give one constructive comment and one positive comment.

The third-grade teachers were having the most frustrating time and could not come up with a viable plan. They wanted to maintain the status quo and make it easier for themselves by requesting that they be observed by the principal or the assistant principal as usual. They wanted to be notified three weeks in advance of being observed. This was a grade with veteran teachers who did not take kindly to change.

Donna suggested that the third-grade teachers meet with the staff members who were on her initial committee to discuss the new plan. She wanted them to obtain advice from their colleagues who could intervene positively to help the third-grade teachers agree to an acceptable format. Then she wanted these teachers to meet with her.

Two weeks later, Donna talked to the third-grade teachers about their new plan. They wanted to be videotaped and no one was to see it other than themselves. They would then watch it and note how successful the lesson was. Donna had one addition to this plan. She wanted to meet with each teacher separately to ask two questions: What did they think was positive? What was one thing they could do to improve? They agreed.

QUESTIONS

1. What guidelines could Donna have provided for the teachers prior to the grade meetings?
2. How could the teachers' final plans be effective for the instructional process?
3. How would the principal be able to evaluate whether the new observation format was working successfully for the students?

COMMENTS

Donna could have provided guidelines for the grade meetings. She could have referred to recent research. And she could have discussed how other schools have used the new model for observations. Perhaps she could have suggested that the teachers talk to teachers in other schools that are using this model. Maybe there could be a visitation program for teachers in her school to observe the teachers in other schools using the new process. Donna could have referred to state or district plans about how to enable teachers to take greater responsibility in their own evaluations. Lastly, she could recommend that the staff go to conferences to hear about teacher empowerment along these lines.

The teachers' final plans can only be effective if they take this approach seriously and see it as an opportunity to improve. They need to be able to recognize that they are being treated as professionals and should see this as a serious effort by the administration to give them greater control over their own improvement. If they look at themselves in an objective manner and perceive what is going well and what needs to be strengthened, this will be an effective process. Their sensitivity and desire to understand that teaching is an art that can constantly be improved is vital. Now they have a wonderful opportunity to evaluate themselves and implement changes in their instruction, which will make them better teachers.

The best way for the principal to see that the new procedures are working is to do a walkthrough every day at different times of the day. Another way to evaluate the new format is to talk to the teachers and ask them to indicate how they feel they are changing for the better in their instruction. Information from parents can also be an indication of improvement. Sometimes talking to the students is another way to evaluate if instruction is improving.

However, the way one asks the questions to parents and students could lead to either a helpful response or one that ends up angering teachers.

Empowering teachers is a powerful tool to help teachers feel better about themselves and their profession and realize that seeking improvement does not necessarily mean that one is unsatisfactory or weak. It can mean that everyone has a chance to take the lead to help oneself to be even better.

Chapter Thirty

The Good Parents' Association President

Darlene Hammond was the ideal parents' association president. The principal and teachers in the Oak Avenue School loved her because she was kind, helpful, and most of all fair-minded. Darlene was available to do photocopying, assisting with lunch or yard duty if needed, and she readily helped with auditorium programs when teachers called upon her. She even went on field trips when a teacher other than her own children's teachers needed an additional parent to chaperone the youngsters.

Darlene worked on many fundraisers and collected more money for the school than any other previous parents' association president. She worked hard, publicized what the fundraiser was all about, and encouraged every parent to pitch in to help and purchase items.

Darlene was an active member of the school leadership team and she was a major asset. She encouraged the principal, Florence Hadley, to find out what was needed by the teachers in advance so she could get the parents who came to the meetings ready to support what the school needed. Darlene did not engage in any of the political infighting that she had heard about in other schools. She did not want the committee to take sides and become power hungry individuals. Instead, Darlene sought to get real solid things accomplished so the children would benefit from the work the committee did.

Sometimes there were complaints from parents about the teachers, which she handled in a most positive way. She would meet with the principal and tell her about the complaints. Then Florence would meet with the teachers and they would come up with a viable response that satisfied everyone. For example, several parents complained that substantive research projects were assigned to the upper grade students just before a holiday week. Parents said that they did not want to have to spend the entire holiday in the library with their youngsters. Nor did they want their children sitting at the computer all week. Many parents wanted the youngsters to have time to play with friends or go on local or long distance trips with their families. This was brought up a week before a school leadership committee meeting. Florence called a meeting with several influential teachers and discussed it in a calm manner. The teachers realized that major projects should either be assigned well before the vacation or after the vacation, but not the day before. The teachers said they would like to be the ones to bring up the issue at the next school leadership committee meeting. Florence called Darlene and she agreed completely. Darlene convinced the other parents that the teachers would be embarrassed at the meeting if parents brought up this topic. Since the problem was going to be solved to their satisfaction, it didn't matter who initiated the discussion as the teachers would no longer assign long projects just prior to a vacation. The parents on the committee agreed.

This is the proactive behavior that Darlene did best. She could smooth the way for any divisive issue that might be uncomfortable for any constituency. When Darlene was going to have a speaker at the parents' association meeting who might talk about a sensitive topic, she would tell the faculty representative. In this way several teachers could attend the meeting and explain their side of the story. On one occasion, Darlene invited a speaker to talk about proper nutrition for the children. Darlene informed the teachers that some of them might want to attend the meeting to hear what the nutritionist had to say about snacks in the classroom because a few of the teachers were having a difficult time and children were bringing whatever snacks they enjoyed. Florence thought the teachers should attend, and she sent out a memo expressing support for attendance at the meeting.

The meeting for one moment seemed tense when a parent shouted, "Those teachers let the children eat whatever they want." The teachers became quite angry, and just when they were about to respond in anger, Darlene stood up and suggested that the speaker comment. "If the parents wish to avoid having the children eat the wrong snacks in class, all they have to do is send in healthy foods. I have a list of what you should send in to the school. Parents, adhere to this list and your children will be eating healthy foods in their classrooms at snack time," the speaker suggested. Florence was ecstatic that the situation was defused. Her teachers did not have to get into a confrontational situation with the angry parents. Once again, Darlene saved the day.

QUESTIONS

1. How can the principal and the teachers thank Darlene for her support and determined advocacy?
2. Why is a "good" parents' association president so important to a school?
3. What could the principal and teachers do to get another "good" parents' association president after Darlene concludes her term?

COMMENTS

The principal and the staff could do many things to recognize the wonderful assistance a helpful parents' association president was providing. There could be a breakfast in his or her honor. The president could be awarded a plaque at the graduation ceremony. He or she could be recognized at a faculty conference in which many teachers could share laudatory remarks. Whatever the occasion, it is important to show gratitude to people who go out of their way to be helpful to the staff.

A helpful parents' association president is vital to a school. He or she works hard fundraising so the school can purchase supplies it might not otherwise be able to obtain. Sometimes these supplies are necessary items, and sometimes they are assembly programs or special materials for the gifted or the remedial youngsters. In addition, a helpful parents' association president can stop rumors from spreading. Rumors sometimes take a great deal of time to quell. By stopping them early, much time, energy, and aggravation is avoided.

A helpful parents' association president can also provide information about new programs. He or she can tell how the community and the parents might react to them so they can be modified before implementation to make them popular and received well by the parents. Next, the helpful parents' association president can be a wonderful vehicle for keeping the school board and the community at large informed about the positive achievements of the school.

The principal and the teachers are supposed to stay out of the electioneering process when the parents vote for their parents' association president. However, they can informally encourage good parents to run. The principal can encourage a member of the executive board to run. The principal can ask the current president to seek out people who would be positive and helpful. This is a delicate matter, so interference with the election is inappropriate. But a negative parent can be so hurtful to the cause of the school that it is imperative for the principal to do subtle things to get the very best person installed as president.

Chapter Thirty-one

The Petulant Parents' Association President

Every once in a while a school staff experiences a parents' association president who is abrasive. She or he can make coming to work a frustrating experience. When a principal and teachers have to deal with such a person, life at work is permeated with fear, anxiety, and demoralization. Time spent thinking about the aggravation caused by the parents' association president takes away attention from instruction. Innovation and creativity are limited. The time and energy spent being concerned with the words and actions of such a person can cause a staff to feel physically ill and drain them mentally.

When Harriet Barnes became the parents' association president of the Lakefront School, Principal Barry Harrison and teacher representative Betsy Diamond knew they were going to a have a year of aggravation and agitation. Harriet had a reputation in the school as one who instigated arguments by exaggerating situations to various parties. She was a natural for being in the middle or starting an altercation and then suddenly backing away and allowing the contenders to fight with each other. Harriet often used inferences in such a negative way that she would stir up issues that should never have been a problem. Somehow she made every situation in which she was involved become 1,000 percent worse.

In the first month of her first year as parents' association president, Harriet began by complaining that no parents or relatives of the children should be allowed to enter the building the first few days of school because "terrorists" could sneak in with the crowd. Discussions took place in which Barry and Betsy explained that plenty of staff and aides and security guards were around to watch and supervise the children. The administration did not make any headway with Harriet. After one week Barry and the union leader met with others and drew up a student safety plan. A letter was sent out to all parents in advance of carrying out the procedures.

The next morning Harriet met at the school with three other parents and demanded that parents be allowed to have full access to the school anytime they wanted. Harriet went into a tirade about the fact that the school belonged to the community and limiting their access to auditorium programs, visits with teachers, parent programs, and special exhibit days was not sufficient. Harriet argued that parents should be allowed to come and go as they pleased whenever their children were in the building. Barry and Betsy finally won out on this issue but they were drained, and the first month of school was not yet over.

In November, Harriet met with Barry to discuss a problem she heard about in the school. It seemed that on at least one occasion a substitute teacher gave out too much homework. Barry investigated the complaint and found it to be valid.

Harriet demanded that a policy be set up in which teachers who are absent, no matter what the reason for the absence, contact the substitute and make certain that the homework never exceeds the prescribed guidelines for the grade. Barry met with a group of teacher representatives. He informed Harriet that the school homework policy was in place and it worked well almost all of the time. In his communication to Harriet, Barry said this one mistake by a new substitute should not make the school change its adequate homework policy, which had worked well for years.

Harriet went to the superintendent and said that Principal Harrison was not being open to suggestions, especially when harm was being done to the children. Barry called in to meet with Superintendent Johnny Masters. In his office Barry explained his side of the situation. He was accompanied by five teachers. They all assured Superintendent Masters that this school had many exemplary policies in place, and even though once in a while human error occurred, the homework policy should not be changed. Since the homework policy was in accord with the plan originally set up by headquarters, the superintendent backed the principal and the teachers completely. But the aggravation that this caused was disturbing to the principal and the teachers.

Incidents such as these occurred repeatedly. The principal and the teachers decided that they were going to do the right things at all times, which is what they had been doing. They were going to keep their cool and they were going to respond to Harriet with respect and courtesy but hold their ground where they believed she was in error. Harriet was allowed to continue with her two-year term. But other parents revolted and at the end of the two years, a new parents' association president was sworn in. Parents throughout the school and the community realized that Harriet was a troublemaker and an irritant and she distracted everyone from doing what each needed to do for the children. Countless parents contacted teachers and the principal and provided moral support for them. They expressed appreciation for the hard work they were doing for the youngsters and were empathetic with regard to the anger and hostility Harriet had caused in the school and community. In the end it was the parents, teachers, and the principal who won because they continued to do what was right. They persevered and were fortunate enough to have a new president who was wonderful, thoughtful, sensitive, positive, and cooperative.

QUESTIONS

1. What strategies can the administration and the teachers undertake to survive abrasive parents?
2. Why are some parents abrasive?
3. Can anything be done by the school staff to encourage positive parents to run for the leadership position of the parents' association?

COMMENTS

As long as the administration and the teachers are doing the very best they can and doing the right things, they can survive abrasive, hurtful parents. Administrators and teachers need to stay calm during meetings with these parents. They must realize that they are good people and that they know what they are doing and that they constantly attempt to improve. When abrasive parents demand that they do something wrong, they must stand firm and continue to use good judgment. When abrasive parents challenge them, they must be able to show what actions they have taken and prove that they were acting in the best interests of the children. The abrasive parents will eventually leave when their children graduate. Life has to go on in the school for the sake of the youngsters.

Parents become angry and abrasive for wide and various reasons. Often the reasons have nothing to do with the administration and the teachers. There are parents who have major personal problems and they take these problems out on the school because all too often schools are sitting targets. Educators have to listen to them and treat them with respect. We cannot just toss them off and send them away. Parents have a right to be heard by the school staff, the central office, and the school board. At first they may seem to be getting away with the belligerency. But after awhile everyone catches on.

Some parents enjoy a feeling of power when they spread rumors and lies. For a while it seems as if they were receiving attention. But as time passes everyone recognizes that they are difficult to say the least. Parents are emotional when it comes to their children. They want their children to succeed and to be the best. Some parents get upset when test results and school report card results are announced. Instead of accepting the results and thinking about what they can do to help their children, some parents find it easier to chide the administration and the teachers.

While teachers and the administration refrain from actively engaging in the affairs of the parents' association, it is important to identify parents who are positive and wish to do good things for the school. In schools where there is a great deal of politics and intrigue and parents behaving unethically, the principal has an obligation to encourage good people to be active in the parents' association leadership. They can do this informally when they meet and talk with parents. They can encourage them to take a strong role for the sake of the school and the children. In cases where parents initiate fundraisers and donate very little money to the school, the administration and the teachers need to ask questions as to where the money is allocated within the school. In cases where it is suspected that the parents' association is stealing funds and not donating to the school, it is important that this be reported to the central office and the authorities.

Chapter Thirty-two

Hands-On Science

Visitors to the Andrew Jackson School were always taken immediately to the classroom of Ethel Brook. Upon entering Ethel's room one often saw active children talking eagerly among themselves as they helped one another with their science experiments. The students carefully used the materials, moved about the room to take or return scientific instruments, and recorded their findings on data sheets.

The Andrew Jackson School was fortunate to have numerous teachers who believed in encouraging movement in the room as the youngsters actively participated in learning. The teachers in this school seemed to work as one unit while carrying out their various educational lessons in separate rooms.

Ethel had been teaching science for five years, and each year she became increasingly more knowledgeable. Prior to teaching science, Ethel had taught third grade. Although she loved teaching third grade, after eleven years she felt she needed a change.

The change came when she saw a vacancy notice at the end of one year and she applied for this specialist teaching position. Once the job was hers, she energized herself into a dynamo. She went back to college and took a night class in "Teaching Science." She spoke to her principal about having a science specialist come to her room to demonstrate the best methods of teaching science. She quickly learned how to teach science using the scientific method. She went to local workshops and joined a national science association.

Students in Ethel's room quickly learned the steps of the scientific method and often referred to a sheet with the scientific method steps. Most loved the last step in which they noted and explained the conclusions found from their experiments.

Teaching science was not easy at first for Ethel. The major problem she had was materials. A science consultant from the superintendent's office met with her early on and gave her lists of materials she would need. Next, she requested that the parents' association fund the purchases. The parents ran a book sale and raised nearly $800 for science supplies. An additional $200 came from the principal's budget.

Ethel communicated with the librarian and the reading and classroom teachers so she could tie her lessons into what others were teaching. They, in turn, sought to align their instruction with that of Ethel. The consistency of lessons gave the students much satisfaction.

QUESTIONS

1. What makes Ethel Brook an effective teacher?
2. How can an administrator recognize Ethel's accomplishments without alienating the rest of the staff?
3. What safety concerns do science teachers need to be alert for?

COMMENTS

Ethel was effective because of her commitment and enthusiasm as well as her willingness to learn the best methods for instructing the youngsters. Her dedication and sincerity were evident in that she could trust the students to move about the room and utilize hands-on activities that made science instruction fun for them as well as meaningful. The fact that she took considerable time to learn about the latest techniques for the teaching of science was significant. It is also important to note that she was assertive in obtaining the proper materials to make the program work.

An administrator can compliment her, send her congratulatory notes, and call her in to the office to privately tell her how wonderful and effective her work is. If the parents' association or the central office has a Teacher of the Year award she could be nominated for this honor. In addition, after visiting her room it would be a good idea to mention to her something wonderful that was noted. Of course, it would not be good politics to publicly overdo the compliments because the other teachers might become jealous. Even though Ethel might deserve the accolades, the other teachers are human and they could feel slighted if the administrators publicly gave her favorable remarks too often. It could also be detrimental to staff morale.

Regardless of how effective and popular the instruction process is, it is vital that teachers be vigilant for the safety of the students. Pupils who take the materials need to be monitored. The use of the materials should be sharply watched, and, of course, it is important to supervise their return to the proper buckets or baskets. Science teachers have a major responsibility to ensure that all materials are used safely and the students are instructed in the use of materials for each step of the lesson. In cases where classes or individuals do not follow directions carefully and are possibly in danger of hurting themselves or others, precautions need to be taken with regard to what type of lessons and materials should be used.

Chapter Thirty-three

Innovative Staff Development

Lynne Weinstein, principal of the Edison School, was elated as she drove home from a principals' training conference. She had just participated in a wonderful experience. The workshop leader, Howard Elkert, was an expert on using the same objectives, procedures, and activities with average and below-average students as one would use with gifted students.

Howard spoke, demonstrated, modeled, and shared research results of average and below-average pupils who made wonderful progress when taught as if they were bright students. He talked about teaching students to "learn how to learn." This related to teaching youngsters skills they needed to conduct research, ask questions, and locate appropriate materials.

Another marvelous topic he spoke about was thinking skills. He discussed how important it was to teach higher-order thinking skills to the average and below-average student. Lynne was pleased to hear that through consistent and patient instruction, average and below-average pupils could make fabulous progress utilizing higher-order thinking skills and be able to perform many tasks like bright youngsters did.

Lynne decided to have her teachers trained to work with average and below-average students with these high expectations as part of their instructional planning.

Lynne's problem was when she would be able to have this training session. She came up with an innovative plan. The parents had complained at several parents' association meetings that the youngsters needed more "socialization time." Lynne remembered that one parent suggested to "Let them play in the playground in the nice weather. Kids today are pressured with academics."

Lynne called her superintendent and then she called the parents' association president. She told them both that in June she was going to have the teachers trained to teach higher-order thinking skills. She said her plan was to have the students go to the schoolyard field to have organized games or just to socialize for two hours while the school's teacher of the gifted led a workshop. She said the two hours for the children to be outside would yield years of higher expectation instruction for all students in the school.

The superintendent and the parents' association president heartily endorsed the plan. So the teachers met in the school library. The youngsters went to the playground.

A parent living nearby saw many youngsters in the field. Although everything seemed orderly, pleasant, and calm, the parent called a school board member. Soon two school board members raced to the school.

"What's going on?" asked one school board member.

"Where are the teachers?" the other asked Lynne.

Lynne explained that the physical education and computer teachers and many aides were watching the children. She then told them what was happening in the library. "Children will benefit from what the teachers are learning today for many years to come." She escorted the two school board members into the library.

As the three of them entered, the teacher of the gifted was demonstrating a technique that could be used to enhance the ability of the average and below-average students. Teachers in the audience were heard to say things such as "This is fabulous!" "I will start using these ideas tomorrow." "I always believed that all youngsters can learn higher order thinking skills. Now I know how to do it."

QUESTIONS

1. Is it fair to let youngsters stay in the yard/field for two hours while staff development is in progress? Why or why not?
2. Should we teach higher-order thinking skills to average and below-average students? Why?
3. How will this kind of staff development benefit the youngsters?

COMMENTS

Ideally, the central office would provide staff development days to inform the teachers of new programs and techniques. However, some schools are not fortunate enough to be able to train teachers during the school day. In cases such as this, administrators need to be innovative so they can find time to upgrade the skills of the staff. If the "playground time" can be structured so that it is organized and it is a time of the year that is appropriate, it would be beneficial to the children in the long run to have their teachers trained in the latest techniques and programs. If it is unmanageable and children could be hurt, then other ways need to be found so that there is time to train the staff in exciting and creative ways to teaching the students.

Higher-order thinking skills encourage teachers to have high expectations for children, and, therefore, it is a wonderful idea for teachers to have in their arsenal of methods. In addition, higher-order thinking skills involve many creative and imaginative techniques that are motivating and quite enjoyable for students. With patience and encouragement many average and below-average children can benefit from these methods.

Teachers can use judgment and if the lessons are too difficult for the youngsters, the lessons can be modified depending upon the learning level of the children. Some youngsters will display skills teachers did not believe the children possessed. Some youngsters will be motivated to enjoy these creative lessons, and perhaps the children will transfer this joy to other academic areas. Some students will blossom and show their own creativity and willingness to try to learn innovative things. In a few cases, the work may be too difficult for children and will require much teacher assistance and repetition. Perhaps this type of activity is not appropriate for those few students who find imaginative activities too overwhelming.

Chapter Thirty-four

In-School Suspension

Every principal seeks ways to improve student behavior since every school has youngsters with discipline problems. One year, the Jefferson School had several youngsters who continually misbehaved. Principal Joe Shakers tried calling parents, asked teachers to change instructional techniques for these wayward youths, involved the guidance counselors and psychologists, and even thought about suspensions. While the teachers realized that some punishment was necessary, all agreed that suspension would only give these pupils a day off with no schoolwork. They thought these students would roam the streets and get into trouble.

Joe met with staff members and decided to take these youngsters out of the lunchroom as punishment. One teacher, Etta Vaughn, volunteered to take the troublesome youths to a lunchtime suspension room. Joe called Superintendent Audrey Jenkins to obtain approval for this unusual plan. She indicated it would be fine as long as the suspensions did not include corporal punishment in any way.

Then Joe discussed the in-house suspension design with the parents' association executive board. They agreed as long as the students did not miss any valuable learning time. The children brought their lunches to the room and afterward had assignments to work on.

Students who threw food, cursed classmates or the lunchroom staff, or took personal property from other youngsters were directed to go to the lunchroom suspension program. Once in the program a child could be released if Etta felt, after several conversations with the pupil, that the child was remorseful and indicated sincerely that he or she would behave well in the future.

While they ate and completed the assignments, they listened to music performed by Frank Sinatra. Since this was not corporal punishment as defined by the school policy, it seemed that it would be a soothing experience for the pupils while they worked on specially assigned exercises after eating lunch.

Etta was a big fan of Frank Sinatra, and when he was alive, she went to many of his performances. She had virtually all of his records, tapes, and CDs and listened to them frequently. For her, this volunteer work was a joy to do. All Jefferson School students and even those problematic students behaved well in her presence.

As soon as she played the music, she could see the students squirming. One pupil, Joseph Meyers, raised his hand and asked if she could please put on music that was more contemporary. Jack Smiley suggested that he could bring in tapes for the future in-house sessions. Etta was adamant that this is what they would have to listen to each and every day.

Within a few weeks, the students became better citizens and were able to return to the lunchroom. The soft, relaxing music proved to be something the students preferred not to hear. Their behavior in lunchroom, gym, auditorium, and classrooms showed remarkable improvement. Teachers informed Joe and Etta that the students had made marvelous changes of behavior and even their academic efforts had improved tremendously.

Parents called Joe to indicate that they saw positive changes in attitudes and praised the school for taking decisive and dramatic action to help the pupils who had been struggling. The parents were grateful that the calls now gave them positive information about class work and special projects and what was expected of the youngsters in the near future instead of complaints about their misconduct.

In the faculty conferences, Joe was now able to emphasize academic innovations instead of discipline problems. The in-house suspensions made a great impact on everyone. Teachers felt that something had been done about the problem. Students could see that one could not get away with poor behavior. Joe was proud that he and his staff acted forthrightly and that discipline had improved in a school he cared for very much.

QUESTIONS

1. Was this type of in-house suspension an appropriate response to student misbehavior?
2. Why was it important for Joe to take decisive action when the discipline problem was causing serious concerns?
3. Why was this plan successful? What signals did the students and teachers receive when this plan was agreed upon by the staff and turned out to be quite successful?

COMMENTS

This type of suspension was fair because the youngsters did not miss out on any class work and it sent a signal to the whole school that misbehavior is something that will not be tolerated. It was fair in that they did get to eat their lunch. This suspension procedure kept the students in school and still provided a form of punishment.

If trouble is not stopped in its early stages, it tends to get worse and can reach a point where students are out of control. Then there are major problems that can be overwhelming. When a principal takes decisive action as Joe did, everyone knows that disorderly pupils will not get away with their behavior. This makes the teachers feel they are supported and raises their morale. Decisiveness illustrates to the students that they are not to cause disruptions or there will be consequences. Most often, parents also support strong administrative leadership.

This plan may have succeeded because a strong disciplinarian volunteered to supervise the students in the in-house suspension room at lunchtime. The respect that these pupils had for Mrs. Vaughan could have been a major reason for the success of the program. Perhaps the music played a role in this process. Certainly the students wanted to get back to the lunchroom to be with their friends during the recess. The students throughout the school and the staff received a strong signal that this is a school where students must be serious and behave respectfully and correctly. Because the plan worked so well one would have to think that the school would become an even better place to work and learn.

Chapter Thirty-five

The New Teacher

Educators lose sleep over so many things. When one works with many other human beings, a variety of circumstances may occur that can cause significant stress. Perhaps one of the most nerve-wracking instances is when a teacher calls the school the Friday before school opens and explains she is moving out of town. When this teacher has been successful, popular, and has maintained a superb reputation, it is even more disturbing because it is not easy to find a replacement just prior to the opening of the new school year.

Principal Barney Whitaker was sitting at his desk Friday at 1 P.M. just prior to Monday's opening of school for the new year. He had the schedules all set. He had completed assignments of teachers and class placements. He had finalized plans for the distribution of materials and books in place. He had a smile on his face as his secretary, Martha Jensen, walked into his office. When Barney saw the look on Martha's face, he knew she did not have good news for him.

"Mary Lou Watkins is on the phone and she wants to talk to you," Martha stated.

"Is something wrong?" he asked.

"Yes. But you talk to her and she'll tell you herself," replied Martha.

"Barney, you know I love working at the Baker Street School," Mary Lou indicated.

"I certainly do. And I also know you have done outstanding work here for seventeen years," Barney responded.

She told him she would have to quit immediately. Her husband was offered a fantastic job in a distant state and they would have to move in two weeks. Barney was devastated. One of his best teachers was leaving and he had no time to find a satisfactory replacement. How could he replace a wonderful veteran teacher who gave total commitment to the children and to the school for so many years?

Mary Lou was loved by all her students for her creativity and instruction that taught them to think and participate actively in class lessons. Mary Lou was respected by the parents who sought to have their children placed in her class every year. And her colleagues would miss her because she helped them in so many ways. She cooperated with them when they needed ideas for plays, trips, and exciting lessons. When bulletin boards were assigned, Mary Lou could be counted on to provide patterns, expressions, key words, and art inventions that even the most experienced teachers would use. He wondered who would be there to answer their questions with such quick and relevant responses?

Barney quickly recovered from his thoughts to wish her well and to tell Mary Lou that if she needed a reference for a job in her new state she could count on a glowing one from him. He began to worry.

Barney called the headquarters office and was told to inquire of the student teachers if any of the outstanding ones were available for work. Barney talked to Nadia Pariss. She has done marvelous work with the two classes she taught. Unfortunately, she had accepted a job elsewhere already. He then called Lola Bensen. He knew she was not of Mary Lou's caliber but she showed fine effort and seemed to be quite dedicated and sincere. He felt whatever weakness she had could be compensated by the fact that she wanted to improve and do a good job.

Barney felt at this late date he did not have the luxury of time to continue calling. It was 1:30 and he had to hire a teacher forthwith. Monday was approaching rapidly. He asked the fourth-grade teachers to come to his office. He told them what had just occurred and he asked them to do whatever they could between now and Monday to get Lola ready for her class. He also said that Lola would be coming in shortly and he wanted them to meet with her so she can get copies of the teachers' manuals and any other materials they could find for her to review over the weekend.

When Barney visited Lola's class Monday morning it looked like she was trying very hard to relate to the children and to teach appropriate concepts. She was struggling, however, and he asked her to come to his office after school. He told her not to worry because he wanted to give her some helpful advice and to set up a program that would enable her to eventually be a fine teacher.

QUESTIONS

1. What else could Barney do at this late date to locate a more satisfactory teacher?
2. What could he do to help the newly assigned teacher?
3. What long-term plans could be set up in order for Lola to become a master teacher?

COMMENTS

Barney could have called his colleagues to see if any of them had laid off any teachers due to lower pupil enrollments or whether they knew of any outstanding teachers that were available. Barney could have asked the headquarters personnel department if any excellent teachers were on its list to be hired. He could have asked several of his teachers who might have friends on leave and may wish to return to work. He could have asked his secretary to bring him the file with names of people he had interviewed during the past year in case of just such a circumstance. Lastly, Barney could have asked Mary Lou or other teachers if they knew of substitutes who had covered classes the previous year and taught satisfactorily.

With Lola now in place, Barney could assign a buddy teacher to orient her to the grade as well as to school rules and procedures. He could set up a team of teachers and provide time for them to help her instruct the youngsters effectively. He could ask a strong disciplinarian teacher to work with her to model how to maintain proper order in the classroom and to demonstrate how pupil involvement need not be chaotic. He could assign the new teacher to observe senior teachers once or twice a week for several weeks. He could ask an excellent teacher to do demonstration lessons with her class. He could videotape her as she teaches and let her watch herself and then evaluate how she felt she taught the lessons. He could recommend readings from journals and magazines to help her see the trends in education. Barney could meet with her every day for the first few weeks to help her with problems as he sees them during his walkthrough visits. In addition, he could send her to headquarters for conferences or to meet with specialists after school. He could also ask specialists from headquarters to come to her room and meet with her, demonstrate lessons for her, and also to listen to her concerns. Perhaps there are in-service meetings and local educational association conferences that would be relevant for her. Barney could talk to her about how to respond to parent concerns, create bulletin boards, plan trips, and teach motivating lessons that fit into the district's curriculum guidelines. He could assign a teacher to work with Lola for whole days or several half days. Most of all, Barney needs to convey what is expected of her in clear terms, and he needs to give her confidence especially when she has had a difficult day. Barney must listen to her and allow her to express what she is experiencing.

Barney should invite Lola to join appropriate committees where she can have input and perhaps make suggestions because a new person may bring ideas and skills to the school that can benefit a program. Also she might be able to view happenings in a new light that bring a fresh approach to a committee. Barney must be sure Lola receives all the necessary memos and paperwork, perhaps assign another teacher to help her to complete her paperwork accurately and within a reasonable time. Lola should be receiving feedback in an ongoing, constructive manner by Barney and perhaps by other teachers so she can constantly improve. She should be involved in child guidance meetings so she can gain an understanding of how to respond to the needs of unruly or unmotivated students. There should be a system in which there is an ongoing dialogue with Lola to seek help when needed and receive suggestions. She should be given support and a mechanism should be in place for her to express her concerns and needs. She also should have sufficient books to use with the youngsters and she should be given advice on how to utilize all materials.

Lastly, a mentor should be provided to assist the new teacher. The mentor should observe her teach and meet regularly to discuss the instructional practices and problems she is experiencing. Also it is important to listen to the new teacher's concerns and to address them with specific assistance, techniques, and responses in a timely fashion. The mentor should also arrange intervisitations for Lola. If the other teacher agrees, the mentor should sit in on the demonstration lesson and discuss with Lola the strengths of the lesson that she could emulate. The mentor should do demonstration lessons with the new teacher's class and model specific practices that relate to the needs of the new teacher to improve instruction and interpersonal relations with the youngsters.

Chapter Thirty-six

Ongoing Assessment

The most enjoyable part of Principal Henry Washington's day was visiting the classrooms. He loved to see the youngsters eagerly working on projects, responding to questions, and working in cooperative groups. As he went from class to class in the Roosevelt Elementary School, he would notice numerous positive techniques and activities. Often he would write notes at the end of the day and leave the complimentary memos in the letterboxes of the teachers.

Every now and then he would witness an event or behavior he did not agree with. If it was something a child had done, Henry would converse with the teacher to see how he could support the teacher so as to assist with improving the poor behavior of the student.

If Henry was displeased with a lesson a teacher was teaching, he would write the teacher a note and ask him or her to see him privately in his office. Henry would listen to the teacher and make suggestions so that type of lesson could be more effective.

On a recent day, Henry called a first-year teacher, Rosa Chaves, into his office. "Rosa, I know you are a first-year teacher," he said. "But I have noticed some truly remarkable practices you conduct. Although I have been an educator for more than twenty years, I want to ask you about your absolutely sensational ongoing assessment."

Rosa was flattered and speechless. She thought that Principal Washington had asked her to come to his office about something she had done wrong. As a relatively new teacher, she was not aware that Henry was more likely to call teachers for a meeting to compliment than to criticize them.

"What exactly do you want me to explain?" asked Rosa Chavez.

"I notice that you are always assessing student progress. You do it before a unit or lesson, during instruction, and constantly while they are working independently. And I think it is fabulous," Henry complimented her.

"Tell me about it," he went on further.

"Well," she began, "I am not sure if it came from student teaching, or conferences I attended, or readings I have done, or from observations of teachers in the school, or instinctively, or just a combination of all of them. But if you want my explanation, here it is. It is made up of eight practices I adhere to:

1. Feedback must be timely—as soon as or after the work is done.
2. Feedback must not be ambiguous. It should be clear, practical, and specific.
3. Feedback must be relevant and each child has to realize and perceive its importance.
4. Feedback which is critical should have some praise so as not to devastate the individual.
5. Feedback must be understandable so the student knows precisely what he or she did wrong and what he or she needs to do to correct that skill or habit or concept.
6. Feedback must be fair and not overly critical.
7. Feedback has to be accepted. The student has to know that he or she made a mistake.
8. Lastly, I try to encourage each student so that he or she knows the errors and works with much interest and energy to do better work."

"Wow," said Henry. "I am impressed."

QUESTIONS

1. How can a principal use a talented new teacher to share her ongoing assessment practices without embarrassing the veteran teachers?
2. What makes some teachers instinctively natural professionals?
3. What qualities does Henry possess to want to learn from someone with so much less experience?

COMMENTS

Henry could implement a program in which teachers share experiences with other teachers. He could do this at faculty conferences or at staff development meetings. He could plan the meetings with a group of teachers, and he could begin with the more experienced teachers who are recognized by the staff as having effective ideas to share. Eventually he could call upon a new teacher to share his or her techniques with the staff.

Veteran educators can identify teachers with outstanding potential in a short time. These soon-to-be master teachers relate positively to the children and provide them with meaningful assignments, explain thoroughly before the youngsters are asked to do independent work, and stop inappropriate behavior before it becomes a major distraction to classroom learning.

Henry, obviously, is a principal who is not afraid to say he can learn from his staff. He also is someone who truly cares about the educational process and wants his school to continuously become a more effective learning center. Henry knows that involving the staff can make the school better. He knows that when teachers share their best practices, everyone benefits, especially the students.

Chapter Thirty-seven

Social Studies Instruction

Indira Gupta was full of trepidation as she opened the door to the office of Alice Johnson, assistant principal of the Washington School.

"Come on in," called out Alice. "Have a seat."

"Did I do something wrong today when you visited my room?" asked Indira.

"No, no, no, no," responded Alice Johnson.

Alice had visited Indira's room for several days in a row as she had done with all the other teachers in the school. When she visited the social studies class, she noticed a pattern in which Indira was imparting facts about the U.S. Civil War. Alice saw that the children were sitting quietly and listening but not participating.

Alice Johnson started the meeting by complimenting Indira for her beautiful room with creative pupil work on the bulletin boards. She then expressed satisfaction with the preparation the teacher had given for the lessons. Although Indira had been in the United States for only six years, she spent considerable time learning U.S. history. The facts she presented were accurate and important. After many accolades, Alice proceeded to help Indira become a more proficient teacher of social studies. Alice suggested that her lessons start with an exciting motivation in which she would get the children fully involved by asking thought-provoking questions. She could show illustrations or use copies of an original newspaper to encourage the youngsters to be part of the lesson. She stated that anecdotes about the period could be used to raise the level of interest. She also explained this motivation period should last no more than five or ten minutes.

Then Alice explained how the next part of the lesson could maintain the interest of the students. Indira could show the children how to research the Civil War and provide small groups with materials to enable them to be totally involved in their own learning. Alice suggested that Indira circulate around the room while the children were working on an activity and explain what they needed to do.

Indira said that she had been trained in her country to lecture the children, and she expected they would able to repeat facts back when she tested them. She said that it was difficult for her to use student activities because when they worked in groups the children became noisy.

Alice said that in this school noise that was constructive was very much accepted. She or the new principal would not be upset if they visited the rooms and saw the students working in groups and talking among themselves. Indira said she would try the suggestions and hopefully the new methods would be more satisfying to the class and help them learn more effectively.

Lastly, Alice requested that Indira use trial and error to give the youngsters an opportunity to report to the rest of the class what new information they learned and how the information was acquired.

"Try various techniques to see which ways of reporting seem to work best," she urged.

QUESTIONS

1. What are the weaknesses of the teacher-dominated lesson?
2. How was Alice helpful in making Indira a better teacher of social studies?
3. What can Alice do if Indira is unable or unwilling to accept the suggestions offered?

COMMENTS

The teacher-dominated lesson does not allow for students to search for information themselves and to actively seek to learn. By sitting still it is harder to learn and to remember because the teacher cannot judge if the pupils are listening and learning or if they are merely sitting quietly and daydreaming. Students remember best when they find new information by themselves. It is true that in the past administrators sought to have quiet classrooms by encouraging teacher-dominated lessons to create a silent atmosphere. Recent research concluded that when students are talking among themselves about what they are learning, they understand more efficiently and remember more. When they fully participate they enjoy the lesson more and feel more productive and responsible for their learning. Often this leads to better behavior for the pupils because it encourages them to be focused and disciplined.

One of the ways to improve instruction in a school is for the administrators, teacher trainers, mentors, and coaches to visit the classes to view the teachers practice their craft. Soon after the informal observations, there should be a meeting in which the observer and the teacher sit down and discuss in detail the pattern of the lessons. Since the helping person will be offering advice and often giving suggestions that could be considered critical, it is best if the criticism is constructive and expressed in sensitive terms.

Alice started the meeting with many compliments and this put Indira at ease and made her feel that she was using some fine practices. It also made it easy for Indira to be open-minded and listen for ways she could improve. By putting the teacher in a positive frame of mind the teacher would be intent on hearing and understanding what the helper is saying rather than feeling defensive.

It is now vital for Alice to visit Indira's room during the social studies lessons to see to what degree Indira uses the new methods. It would be hoped that Indira would begin encouraging the students to be active learners and that they would enjoy participating in exciting activities. If Indira fails to employ the new techniques, she may require the services of a coach. The coach may have to teach Indira's class using these new methods. Indira could then observe how hands-on lessons work for herself. In addition, she may need help with acquiring materials to fit this format. Indira needs to be able to evaluate the students' learning to be sure that within the new framework the students are acquiring important concepts and skills. Once Indira has had a significant amount of support, she should be given handwritten notes if she is still not implementing it or if she is unable to change. Then other interventions may need to be provided. Perhaps a specialist in social studies could be brought in to help her. Perhaps another teacher in the grade could show her how to teach using this method.

If this still does not induce Indira to use the method, a formal meeting should take place and a letter indicating the decisions made should be given to Indira. If she is still unable to teach effectively, her performance should be documented more formally in writing and she should be given a period of time to improve as specified in the letter. Perhaps she should be replaced as a social studies teacher and she could exchange classes with another teacher. Lastly, if the problem persists, she needs to be written up, given much support, and eventually encouraged to leave teaching. If necessary, formal charges can be brought and the district or county could seek to have her discharged. This is a lengthy process, but with much paperwork that shows the enormous support provided and the step-by-step procedures taken, perhaps she can be discharged.

Chapter Thirty-eight

A Difference of Styles

In another flurry of mandates emanating from the No Child Left Behind legislation, the Warner Township Board of Education was now requiring each school to implement a math curriculum closely aligned with the standardized tests that tenth-grade students would sit for. Sam Tully, principal at Harbor Hills School in the township, met with Gene Wilson, supervisor of mathematics, to begin program implementation. Sam discussed with Gene the various aspects needed to effectively administer the new curriculum. A partial list included scheduling, teacher training, student selection, course content, materials, assessment measures, budgeting, and effective supervisory practices. Sam was very explicit in his planning with Gene whom he placed in charge of the program.

It soon became apparent to Sam that the math curriculum needed drastic revision. On his daily rounds of classroom visits to assess math instruction, Sam noticed that several teachers understood neither the philosophy behind the program nor the recommended teaching strategies. Worse, students were not engaged in the lessons. As Sam viewed the problem, Gene seemed too aloof and failed to adequately supervise the curriculum.

Sam decided to meet with his longtime supervisor to share his observations and make adjustments in the program. The meeting was critical for several reasons. Sam knew the importance that his boss, Superintendent Ellen Whelan, had placed on the math program as the solution to the problematic test scores at Harbor Hills School. He also knew the need to get Gene to assert more leadership and become more involved in day-to-day decisions of the math department. If he could not motivate Gene, Ellen would surely view the floundering math curriculum as evidence of Sam's failure to supervise his administrative team.

Sam initiated the meeting by thanking Gene for clearing his schedule to discuss the issues and expressed the hope that they could develop a plan to correct program deficiencies. He thanked Gene for his long service to the school that extended over a dozen years or more. Sam suggested that Gene become more hands-on in his dealings with the math teachers and involve himself more in running the department. "Your style may be too laissez-faire, and that's a problem," commented the principal. Gene murmured that his style was not so much laissez-faire as it was collaborative.

Sam then proceeded to outline ideas to help Gene. First, he recommended that Gene register several teachers for an upcoming in-service course on teaching the new math. Second, he invited Gene to link up with Diane Quely, his math counterpart at Brookville School, a neighboring school. By all accounts, the math curriculum was flourishing at Brookville. Third, he offered to set up a series of weekly lunch meetings to discuss program progress. As Sam listed the ideas he was prepared to offer, Gene sat in stony silence and nodded. Sam knew then and there the success or failure of the new math curriculum depended on his next moves. He could not completely rely on Gene's style, whether it be passive, laissez-faire, or collaborative, to lead the effort.

QUESTIONS

1. Compare and contrast the leadership styles that describe Sam and Gene.
2. Which style is more conducive to getting positive results? Explain.
3. How does the superintendent's leadership style impact Sam's own leadership style?
4. Analyze the effectiveness of Sam's approach in dealing with Gene.
5. What other approaches could Sam use to gain Gene's commitment to the math program?
6. Is it fair for the superintendent to judge Sam on the basis of Gene's performance?
7. Role play the meeting between Sam and Gene using different strategies.

COMMENTS

In this vignette Sam recognized the problem, presented his analysis, and developed a response with several ideas to help improve the math program. Yet Gene does not commit to accept Sam's recommendations. Why not?

It may well be that Sam has not allowed Gene to express his feelings on the issues confronting the program. Sam knows very well that he and Gene have different leadership styles, and this has produced a palpable tension between the two of them. Sam is more accustomed to taking on a very direct approach that allows him to remain in charge. This type of approach is generally referred to as command-and-control leadership.

In keeping control of the conversation, Sam has done what many leaders do. They develop on their own an analysis-action plan and simply order implementation. Such an approach may be more suited to the military, where one is expected to dutifully carry out orders with little questioning. Commitment is assumed, and compliance is expected. In education, however, commitment and buying into the leader's ideas cannot be assumed. The workforce of today does not give support and trust too quickly. Rather, the leader must earn the support and trust of the staff. In this case, Gene is a longtime veteran who may not fully subscribe to Sam's methods: direct, straightforward, to-the-point. Sam might earn Gene's support for the new curriculum with a more indirect and collaborative appeal. Instead of presenting his plan as a fait accompli, he may be wise to ask Gene for his diagnosis of what ails the math curriculum and seek remedies from Gene and the math teachers. This strategy is certainly different from Sam's own tendency to make decisions through fiat. That top-down, "thou shalt" approach deprives creative decision making by faculty and may thereby limit faculty support for the new math.

This is a 180-degree turnabout from Sam's initial approach. Under this more collegial approach, the focus has shifted from Sam's directive supervision to Gene's collaborative supervisory style. In seeking Gene's input and that of the teachers, Sam has succeeded in getting Gene to express his views. Sam has begun to validate Gene's professional views and gain greater commitment.

Chapter Thirty-nine

When Pupil Achievement Goes South

Federal and state governments have promulgated policies on testing and school accountability. As part of these requirements, schools must demonstrate annual yearly progress. Any repeated failure to show an increase in student performance can have serious consequences for such a school. More extreme consequences include wholesale transfer of the faculty and even closing the school completely. Earl Rusnak, principal of the Liberty School, hoped to avoid such a fate for his faculty, his students, and, above all, his own career.

After careful study, Earl discovered that while the school had enjoyed a reputation for student achievement over the years, there had been a subtle drop in test scores for a large numbers of students. Earl's analysis showed that minority students from lower socioeconomic backgrounds were not doing well on the standardized tests.

Earl resolved to address the staff on the issue of pupil achievement. After making a convincing PowerPoint presentation at a faculty conference, he sought to tap the talents of several teachers to draft a plan. Earl convened a series of meetings in which he shared various data to illustrate the need for higher student achievement. He even began to discuss ideas about revamping the school's traditional curriculum to make it more appealing to the students.

After considerable discussion and several after-school meetings with the School Improvement Committee over the course of approximately one month, faculty representative Millie Rathgen suggested to Earl that henceforth, teachers should focus on teaching exclusively for the tests. "We'll surely get results if we focus on what the tests require," she stated confidently. In addition to Millie's thoughts, individual teachers spoke of their own concerns about the school's ranking.

John Hawkins bluntly stated, "We have good teachers here but we can't get the results we want because the community and the parents don't give us the support we need."

Phyllis Grant commented, "Our kids have so many emotional needs we must respond to before we even touch the academics. Some of our students do not even have breakfast before school. I wish the tests would measure the dedication and the love we give to our students. The tests are no way to judge a school."

Frank Jessup tried to help Earl with his own interpretation of the pressure to get better results. "Everything runs in cycles, Earl. This too shall pass. Don't beat yourself up over this. We are doing the best we can with limited resources. We have heavy turnover of teachers every year and it takes time to bring the new staff up to speed," said Frank as he put his hand on Earl's arm to reassure him.

QUESTIONS

1. How should Earl address the issues raised by the faculty representative? How should he deal with the comments expressed by John, Phyllis, and Frank?
2. Are there other ways to determine whether a school is doing a good job besides test results?
3. What are some possible factors that might explain poor achievement at Liberty School?
4. How can Liberty School effectively address these factors?

COMMENTS

The debate at Liberty School is a debate that all schools throughout the country continue to have as the mandates of No Child Left Behind legislation are being enforced. At the outset of the debate Earl needs to make it clear to the faculty that in their efforts to resolve the achievement gap, explanations that John, Phyllis, and Frank may offer for poor performance are excuses and rationalizations. Educators today can no longer wail about the lack of community support or little parent involvement as key factors in the downward spiral of pupil achievement. Earl must educate his faculty to the new demands for accountability placed on schools. Those demands call for higher pupil achievement irrespective of socioeconomic conditions or other typical explanations for substandard learning.

Millie's suggestions that faculty should teach to the test also falls short as a strategy for success. Teaching for test mastery measures solely what students are prepared for and not for what they may need to learn through an enriching curriculum. When schools place undue emphasis on test success, they run the risk of converting educational institutions into testing factories whereby success is determined simply on the basis of scores.

As principal Earl has the authority to enact several measures that have strong potential for success. He can hire teachers who possess strong content knowledge and who have the ability and the willingness to promote optimistic expectations for student success. He can assign his most capable teachers to teach those grades that take standardized tests. He can revise the instructional program to include extended blocks of time devoted to literacy improvement. He can organize a professional development plan for faculty that stresses issues of curriculum, instruction, and best practices research that improve teaching and learning. In doing so the plan should be a collaborative one that encourages the participation of teachers like Phyllis, John, and Frank. As faculty representative, Millie occupies a key role in helping to reduce the gap, and she should certainly be included in plans for improvement.

Earl should share with faculty the research on the achievement gap that identifies several variables under the control of the school. These variables have a clear impact on student success. A rigorous curriculum that challenges student thinking is one variable associated with student achievement. Another is the presence of teachers with at least five years' experience. Minority and low-income students in failing schools are more likely to be taught by inexperienced teachers who have not mastered their craft. Teacher preparation also ranks as an important correlate of achievement because minority students are more likely to be taught by uncertified teachers. According to Arthur Wise, president of the National Council for the Accreditation of Teacher Education, "the dirty little secret is that there are large numbers of unqualified individuals teaching, and they are disproportionately assigned to teach children of color and children from impoverished backgrounds" (cited in Grossman, Beaupre, and Rossi 2001). The end result of all these school-related factors is inevitable for underachieving youngsters.

A more fundamental challenge to improving student achievement at Liberty may well be the expectations that faculty has for the success of their students. Whether teachers truly believe that students can learn has a strong influence on their performance (Rosenthal 2002; Weinstein 2002). In confronting this issue, however uncomfortable it may be, Earl needs to engage faculty in a serious dialogue. The research on expectations as a factor in achievement should be explored.

As important as test results may be to measure a school's performance, is it fair to judge the effectiveness of schools on the basis of standardized tests?

Hardly. Such a measure is too simplistic. While pupil success on tests is a valid criterion to determine school effectiveness, it offers only a partial explanation. Any conclusions about the quality of a school should also consider a variety of other factors: teacher attendance; teacher retention; parent participation in school activities; faculty interest in learning new approaches to teaching and learning; the degree of responsiveness by administration to faculty, parent, and student concerns; the availability of administration around the school and in the community; home-school communication; extracurricular activities for students; comparing each child's test scores to his or her previous test scores; and the existence of meaningful programs for children with special needs.

REFERENCES AND SUGGESTIONS FOR FURTHER READING

Grossman, K. N., B. Beaupre, and R. Rossi. 2001. Poorest kids often wind up with the weakest teachers. *Chicago Sun-Times*[Online], September 7. Available at www.mail-archive.com/science@lists.csi.cps.k12.il.../msg00708.html.

Landsman, J. 2004. Confronting the racism of low expectations. *Educational Leadership* 62 (3): 28–32.

Rosenthal, R. 2002. The Pygmalion effect and its mediating mechanisms. In J. Aronson (ed.), *Improving academic achievement: Impact of psychological factors on education*. San Diego, CA: Academic Press.

Weinstein, R. S. 2002. *Reaching higher: The power of expectations in schooling.* Cambridge, MA: Harvard University Press.

Chapter Forty

A Tug of Conscience

Thanks largely to a genuinely collaborative work environment, the community of Southern Middle School had come to view the school as a desirable school for its students. For many of them, the school and its teachers were the anchor the youngsters needed in a sea of chaos that overwhelmed many of their lives. The vast majority of students received free or reduced lunch due to family poverty. Parents themselves suffered from unusually large unemployment rates, and dysfunction characterized many homes. Child abuse and a violent neighborhood gave the 1,200 adolescent boys and girls at Southern School little hope.

As principal, Sue Hammer supported the faculty in the care they gave to their students. They demonstrated this care in a variety of ways. It was not uncommon, for example, for teachers to take money from their own pockets to buy little extras for their students. When Johnny Ellison came to school every day wearing the same tattered shirt, his teacher, Nicole Carson, made sure to buy him the latest clothing fashion as a birthday gift. Another student, Alex Mann, wanted to play basketball in the local league. When his mom could not afford the registration fees, his teacher arranged for payment.

Stories like these abounded in the community, and the teachers were local heroes for their interest in the well-being of their students. The principal, herself a resident of the Southern community, encouraged this kind of family-school involvement in every way she could. She took pride in the community's description of Southern School as "the school that cares."

Sue knew, however, that her role as principal required more than the caring school community she helped to nurture. With the passage of numerous local policies and state and federal legislation designed to improve school performance, Sue was becoming more conscious than ever of her new role as the chief instructional leader for Southern. She knew she had to develop new programs and initiatives that would lead to higher levels of achievement. The standards movement was being ushered into schools across the country, and Southern School was no exception. As a result of the No Child Left Behind legislation, the federal government, the local board of education, and the general public all demanded greater accountability from its schools.

Sue took this assignment seriously but she continued to feel a tug of conscience. Her heart told her that the social and emotional needs of children should be a priority in the life of the school. After all, her interest in the whole child was precisely the reason she entered teaching after a successful career in journalism. She wanted to be an "impact" leader, as she often described her role as principal. Her head told her something totally different. Unless the school could reverse the southerly course of its scores on standardized tests, she would probably be reassigned to another school as principal. Faculty also would be transferred to other schools in the district, and a new staff would be sent to Southern. As a resident of the community, Sue was determined to find other ways to help her students and their families.

QUESTIONS

1. If you were her adviser, how would you help Sue resolve her dilemma?
2. Is the primary role of educators that of instruction and pupil achievement, or is it the overall growth and development of students into responsible citizens?
3. How can these different roles be meshed?
4. Are teachers who emphasize the social-emotional domain of childhood being responsible educators? Are teachers who believe their primary role to be that of teaching children the academics shortchanging students?
5. Given Sue's focus on providing a warm and safe school environment for her adolescent students, how effective is she as principal?
6. How can Sue begin to reorient faculty, students, and parents to the demand for higher levels of academic achievement?
7. How can Sue begin to refocus her own priorities as principal to reflect the new demands imposed on her?

COMMENTS

Government policies have made schools more accountable for student achievement. The Southern School is no exception. To ignore the learning needs of students, or relegate these needs to lesser importance than their social-emotional needs, is tantamount to educational neglect, regardless of how caring the staff may be.

Sue must use her leadership skills to educate her staff that the mission of schools has now expanded more than ever before. This new mission demands higher levels of pupil achievement with serious consequences for failure to meet goals. She must work with her faculty to redesign school priorities that reflect a renewed commitment to student success.

While stating the new emphasis on achievement and learning, Sue cannot ignore the social-emotional needs of her students. Which role for faculty—instruction or overall student well-being—is more important? An either/or, yes/no response begs the question. As H. L. Mencken observed, for every question there is generally an answer that is right, quick, easy—and probably wrong. Southern School must incorporate the social-emotional and academic needs of students into their improvement plans.

During the shaky periods of youthful adolescence, faculty at Southern School must commit to developing the whole child. One of the most significant indicators of student success is a serious adherence to the middle school philosophy in which all policies and programs are based on the developmental needs and interests of students. Research confirms this idea that higher pupil performance is achieved when there is sustained pursuit of this middle school philosophy.

Sue is fortunate in that she has at her disposal the potential of a caring faculty. The fact that faculty cares about the well-being of Southern students represents a powerful resource to raise achievement levels. So how can Sue and the faculty translate this care to produce results? One possible approach might include the elimination of any tracking system that consigns students to rigid educational caste systems. Another approach is to create a teacher advisory program with a focus on matching each student to an adult advocate. Using an advisory program concept each grade level is guided by a team of teachers who work together to provide a stable and supportive school atmosphere. These groups meet on a regular basis to consider the learning, social, emotional, and physical needs of students and to develop strategies to help students cope with the many issues that confront them. Each student is assigned an adviser who communicates with parents through a regular series of communications.

Teaming for instruction is another approach to help strengthen student learning. Faculty teams plan jointly to coordinate lessons. For example, math and science teachers engage in joint efforts to make these subjects more interesting and relevant to their students. Another team of social studies and language arts teachers may combine to play a strong role in teaching students the skills of reading, writing, and communication.

In a report prepared for the Alliance for Excellent Education, "Reading Next—A Vision for Action and Research in Middle and High School Literacy" (Biancarosa and Snow 2004), a panel of experts recommended fifteen essential components of strong reading instruction for adolescents. Sue and the Southern School community would be advised to consider these elements:

1. Direct, explicit comprehensive instruction
2. Effective instructional principles embedded in content
3. Motivation and self-directed learning
4. Text-based collaborative learning
5. Strategic tutoring
6. Diverse texts
7. Intensive writing
8. A technology component
9. Ongoing formative assessment of students
10. Extended time for literacy
11. Professional development
12. Ongoing summative assessment of students and progress
13. Teacher teams
14. Leadership
15. A comprehensive and coordinated literacy program

The principal should capitalize on another untapped resource, namely, the parents who already support the school. Invite parents to participate in school activities and parent advisory committee meetings. Encourage frequent home-school communication through regular Principal's Pen letters informing parents of school progress and the variety of services offered to students and their families. The principal and staff may wish to hold parent meetings in the community.

Sue has already demonstrated she is a caring leader. She can extend this caring role and become the instructional leader she yearns to be by communicating with students during advisory periods to learn their needs and exhort them to higher performance levels.

REFERENCES AND SUGGESTED READINGS

Biancarosa, G., and C. E. Snow. 2004. *Reading Next—A vision for action and research in middle and high school literacy: A report from the Carnegie Foundation New York.* Washington, DC: Alliance for Excellent Education.
Booth, D., and J. Rowsell. 2002. *The literacy principal.* Portland, ME: Stenhouse Publishers.
Clark, M., K. Shreve, and C. Stone. 2004. Taking stock in children: Collaborating to promote success for low-income secondary students. *NASSP Bulletin* 88 (641): 61–73.
England, C. 2004. *Uphill both ways: Helping students who struggle in school.* Portsmouth, NH: Heinemann Publishers.

About the Authors

Dr. Benjamin Piltch has had extensive experience as a classroom teacher, central office administrator, principal, college professor, and college administrator of an education master's degree program.

Dr. Terrence Quinn's leadership as a school principal earned him nationwide distinction as *Reader's Digest* American Hero in Education. He is currently associate professor of educational leadership at Queens College, New York City.